WHO I WILL BE

Is There Pathos in God?

by

ROBERT WILD

Priest of Madonna House

WIPF & STOCK · Eugene, Oregon

Wipf and Stock Publishers
199 W 8th Ave, Suite 3
Eugene, OR 97401

Who I Will Be
Is There Pathos in God?
By Wild, Robert
Copyright©1976 by Wild, Robert
ISBN 13: 978-1-5326-9244-4
Publication date 5/22/2019
Previously published by Dimension Books, 1976

El-Shaddai, El-Ohim, El-Olam, Yahweh, Melek, Adonai, Kurios, Pantocrator, Lord, Mighty One, All-knowing, Unknowable, Impassible, God of Israel, Father, Blessed Trinity — Father, Son, and Holy Spirit, O Thou of many names and no name, I dedicate this book to You. Guide all who read it to know who You really are for them. I seek your face, which is the echo in me of your seeking mine.

While he was still a long way off,
his father saw him and was moved with
pity. He ran to the boy, clasped
him in his arms and kissed him tenderly.

                              Jesus of Nazareth

TABLE OF CONTENTS

PREFACE 7

1. INTRODUCTION: The Passionless 9

PART ONE   *A PAIR OF GLASSES*

2. Both are Words of God 28
3. Ezekiel and Aristotle 40

PART TWO   *THE JOURNEY*

4. Yahweh 53
5. Father 70
6. The Unchangeable 88
7. The Impassible 105
8. The Unknowable 123

9. CONCLUSION: The Passionate 140

APPENDIX A 160

FOOTNOTES 161

PREFACE

The Spirit of Jesus attracts our hearts to the Father in an infinite variety of ways. Some of these ways are understandable in the light of our backgrounds and temperaments; the rest is lost in the mystery of God's special touch.

Thus, one person is attracted by the awesome mystery of the indwelling Trinity, another by the incredible humanness of the Sacred Heart, another by the Crucified, another by the action of the Spirit who is continually being poured forth by the Lord Jesus, another by the Eucharistic Presence, another by the presence of Christ in the poor. And within all these special attractions are still finer modifications such as joy, expiation, victimhood, childlikeness, love, and so on, there being as many varieties and combinations as there are people.

One of the particular aspects of the Spirit's enticement of my own heart is the feelings or the pathos of God, the subject of this book. Not only is it a modality of my own approach to God: I feel some special vocation both to explore this theme in theology and to try and develop its ramifications for the spiritual life of man. In my own mind, this book is simply the first fruits of that enterprise. Eventually, as God provides the talent and opportunities, I hope to explore as many facets of the feelings of God as possible.

I believe the truth involved in the pathos of God is extremely important for our interior lives. A clarification and deeper understanding of it could immeasurably enrich our relationship with God. I appreciate too that my efforts are not at the deepest level of scholarship and creativity, and that the real in-depth work will be done by others more competent. However, one does what one can! I can at least help to present some of the work being done by others as one way of shedding light on the topic.

Because this is a rather debatable issue, I wish to make it clear that the book represents only my own thinking and should in no way be taken as representing the views of my dear family of Madonna House. We are all, each in our own way, searching to "know God and Jesus Christ whom he has sent," since this will be the content of our everlasting life. This book is part of *my own* search.

Robert Wild
Madonna House, Combermere, Ont.
March, 1976

1. Introduction: The Passionless

Never to be forgotten, to be neglected, to be derided, is the inconspicuous figure in the quiet back room. He sits with head bent, silent, waiting, listening to the commotion in the streets. He is the keeper of the kinds.

Who is he? We do not know. Nor shall we ever. He is a presence, and that is all. But his presence is evident in the last reaches of infinite space beyond man's probing eye. His presence is guessable in the last reaches of infinite smallness beyond the magnification of electron or microscope. He is present in all living beings and in all inanimate matter. His presence is asserted in all things that ever were, and in all things that will ever be. And as his command is unanswerable, his identity is unknowable. But his most ancient concern is with order.

Where a child is born, or a man lies dead; where life must go on, though tragedy deny it; where a farmer replants fields again despoiled by flood or drought; where men rebuild cities that other men destroy; where tides must ebb as tides have flowed; there, see his footprints, there, and there.

He does not care about you, or about me, or about man....

Robert Ardrey, *African Genesis*

In his masterful work, *The Prophets*, the late Abraham Heschel (himself a prophet), described the essence of the prophetic consciousness as the experience of the pathos of God: the prophet felt what God himself was feeling about man and the world. God's pathos was described as his "being in a personal and intimate relation to the world...a living care, a dynamic relation between God and the world...(God's) constant concern and involvement...an emotional engagement."[1]

"Pathos" may be an unfamiliar and little used word for many people. For those more literary minded it may denote a maudlin reaction of sorrow or pity. In this book I would like to restore the word to something of its original meaning, that is, "the ability or quality of being affected." Thus, the word "pathos" will be used to refer to that characteristic of God, portrayed in the scriptures, whereby God is presented as being affected, for better or for worse, by the actions of man and by the course of history. I believe this affectedness is part of the biblical revelation concerning God's relationship to us. I believe also that at the present time it is not adequately understood or given a place in our theology. For the purpose of this book, the words "pathos" "feelings" and "affectedness" will be used synonymously.

You can open countless books today and read of peoples' need for and belief in a God who cares for, suffers and rejoices with humanity, a God who is not indifferent to the cries of distress of his people. "No, I shall never believe in a God...who says and feels nothing about the agonizing problems of suffering humanity."[2]

When reading such statements, it is never quite clear whether the writer, as a Christian, is referring to the humanity of Jesus, is using devotional and poetic language, or is speaking "anthropomorphically" and knows that no one will take him literally. "No one will take him literally." We cannot take him literally because, as everyone knows, God does not change. We do know that God loves us intensely, that he has sent his Son Jesus, and so forth—all the wonderful truths of our faith cry out that God is a Lover of men. But—and this is the common understanding—God can not change. He loves us, cares for us, is intensely concerned about us, yet, God does not change. The purpose of this book is to make a modest contribution to the contemporary, ongoing dialogue concerning this passibility, this pathos of God.

The present writer is fairly aware of his limitations. Our knowledge of God involves many layers of investigation. For the final judgment I bow to the experts. On the other hand, Jesus reveals the Father to all those who seek him with a sincere heart. I would hope to be numbered among these latter. Also, I believe that the pathos of God is one aspect of Jesus' revelation of the Father to his people. With this book I would like to help give voice to this revelation.

My intention is to write a simple book, an uncomplicated book, about a topic that is not simple. I wish to make available to a wider audience what many scholars are writing and thinking about the passibility of God. Scholars, therefore, do not need this book; they will find nothing very new in it. It is designed for a larger audience, and the challenge will be how to present what is not simple in the simplest possible way.

For the issues discussed here are recognized as being far from superficial. They are deep and profound, and their ramifications for our lives with God are far-reaching and marvelous, unspeakably marvelous. They are not matters to be spoken of lightly. Hence, the need to use the findings of many scholars. My intention is to present their findings as popularly as I can without being superficial. I believe that there is already much material available on this subject of the pathos of God. It seemed that a small book was in order, to present some of these findings to a wider audience, in the hope of opening the question to a fuller airing.

Thus, this book is presented not so much as a "proof" of the pathos of God, as a proposal, an outline, a sort of position paper for further discussion. My approach will be to take a closer look at our knowing faculties, using some recent findings on human consciousness and modes of thought. Then, we will take a tour through some of the early centuries to see how these knowing faculties of ours produced different kinds of notions about God. I will elaborate on the fact that there are basically two kinds of knowledge, rational and intuitive, and that each kind has a place in our knowledge of God's characteristics. We hope to show how, in the course of transition from biblical to post-biblical times, the rational element predominated in an inordinate fashion, and some aspects of God (here specifically his feelings) were submerged and neglected in the history of theology. The book, as will readily be seen, is mainly a brief historical study to bolster this contention.

This notion of the pathos and the passibility of God may seem rather outrageous to many Catholics and to other Christians as well. A friendly critic of mine said that this doctrine is not so much outrageous to Catholics as against orthodoxy! It is a serious objection, and something of the question in relation to Church teaching will be said later. Certainly one of the questions in my own mind is how intimately bound up with orthodoxy *is* the doctrine of God's immutability.

While most people probably shuddered at Ardrey's description of the presence lurking in the back room of the universe, and rejected it as a most un-Christian view of the Creator, it is the quasi-thesis of this book that there is in our doctrine of God just such an uncaring element. We can use all the personal and poetic language we wish about God's love for us, but (and this is the big but) when one gets "intellectually serious about it," and starts discussing it with the theologians and philosophers, the answer finally comes: "Yes, God loves us. Still God cannot change." In the serious world of thought and doctrine, the pathos of God is more often in the realm of pious and devotional language—anthropomorphic, if you will. But *really*, God cannot change.

One immediate and obvious objection is that I seem to be equating "pathos" with "change." I am. If words mean anything at all, I do not see how we can have any sort of real pathos, and make any concrete sense out of the biblical intuitions, without some kind of real change in God. And if it is countered that God is really "beyond words" and therefore beyond concepts such as "change" and "immutability"—that he is in a realm where these words and the realities they designate are joined in a perfect synthesis—I would readily agree, *as long as I am then allowed to speak of change in God as well as of immutability*! If one is legitimate, so is the other. If he is in a realm "beyond words," "pathos and change" are as applicable to him as "immutability." But I do not believe that presently "change" is a proper word to use in reference to God. The common teaching is that he is immutable. This, it seems, does not put him "beyond words."

If articles in the *New Catholic Encyclopedia* are any indication of the general thinking, then the general position is that God does not change:

IMMUTABILITY OF GOD

The divine attribute whereby God is said to be completely changeless and unchangeable, and thus different from the changing things of man's experience.[3]

The author's (William Hill, O.P.) treatment of the subject gives no indication that there is any room for the pathos of God.

Likewise, in Church pronouncements throughout the ages, there is no mention of pathos. The Lateran Council (649): "If anyone does not confess properly and truly in accord with the holy Fathers...that the Father, and the Son, and the Holy Spirit are...one God in three subsistences...one and the same Godhead, nature, substance ...uncreated, without beginning, incomprehensible, immutable...." (Denz. 254); the Lateran Council IV: "Firmly we believe and we confess simply that the true

God is one alone, eternal, immense, and unchangeable
...(Denz. 428).4

This book does not intend to respond to all the dimensions of this question; something briefly further on will be said about the development of doctrine. Certainly a complete treatment of this question would require relating the notion of pathos to Church pronouncements.

I do not deny that this notion of pathos is unfamiliar to Catholics. But there have been rumblings. In 1947, the very popular and influential spiritual writer, Father Gerald Vann, O.P., wrote a book called *The Pain of Christ and the Sorrow of God*. In it he wrote: "We know that love cannot but be involved in the suffering of what it loves; but God is love; therefore God cannot but be involved in the suffering of what he loves; but he loves all his creatures; therefore he cannot but be involved in the sufferings of all his creatures. Are we playing with words when we say God suffered? The answer is emphatically no."5

Father Vann tried to answer the problem of suffering in God by viewing it as a problem between time and eternity: suffering for us is "in time" but for God it is "in eternity." In his view, the difficulty is also due to the fact that we cannot hold opposite qualities such as pain and joy in a unity of experience. God can. While it is not clear to me how his approach solves the problem, I believe his intuitions were of the exact same kind as we will be describing throughout this book. At the time of his writing, and using the philosophical categories which were available to him, he stated, as well as anyone, the mystery of pathos with which we are concerned:

> While the mystery of divine pity is temporally expressed in Calvary through the humanity of Christ, it is also eternally and constantly present in the depths of the Godhead, not indeed in the form of suffering as humanity knows it, but as the eternal will-to-share which is no fiction or play upon words but the true involvement of a state of being....

God's cross goes on; and slowly, constantly thwarted by our perversity and blindness and evil but still continuing, the revelation of love's meaning goes on. Evil produces its ineluctable consequences, and the world is drenched in pain; but at every point in time and space where pain has its kingdom, there also are the tears of God, and sooner or later through the tears the soul of the world is renewed.6

I wish I could write like that! I wish I could write like that because this religious intuition of the pathos of God is worthy of great poetry and depth of feeling. The implications of these words by Father Vann are as far-reaching as anything that will be stated in this book. The theme is not entirely new; there are precedents. Father Vann was quoted to put the Catholic reader a bit more at ease!

Yes, there are precedents, many precedents in the hearts of men. For the intuitions of the real affectedness of God—his pathos—have always been in us. It is part of Jesus' personal instruction of his followers concerning their relationship with the Father. Then what is the problem? The problem concerns more the theological and philosophical attempts to speak about this intuition. I believe that our forthcoming intellectual journey through the early centuries will show how this religious and biblical intuition was distorted and not successfully articulated. But before we begin, we would like to take a look at other contemporary recognitions of the problem.

Joseph Donceel, S.J. is a prominent Thomist philosopher and writer—a typical representative of the Thomistic school. His description, therefore, of the basic Thomistic position on the question with which we are concerned portrays the understanding of most Catholics acquainted with the problem on the philosophical plane:

> What is basically at stake here is our conception of the relation which exists between God and his creation. Creation certainly possesses a relation to God. Does God possess a relation to his creation? Scholastic philosophy tends to answer No to this

question. It argues that, since creation is not eternal, such a relation would be a modification, a change in God. But the Pure Act cannot change and no modification is possible in Infinite Perfection. From the creatures to their Creator the relation is real. From the Creator to his creatures the relation is purely mental; it is a relation of reason.[7]

This is the present, common understanding—and it was Donceel's until a short while ago! In the encounter with his students, Donceel met three powerful objections to this traditional notion of the unchangeable God. One was positivism, the idolatry of science. He considers this reason shallow. The second objection was the old problem of evil. The third concerns the devalorizing of human existence and history if God remains completely unaffected by what occurs.

These last two objections Donceel considered serious, serious enough to make him reconsider his position:

> I consider it my duty as a Professor of philosophy, who is deeply convinced of the existence of God and of the deep reasonableness of this conviction, to share it with my students. My experience of the last few years has shown me that young people can even less than I accept the immutable God of traditional theism....This is where the traditional theist will probably call a halt and say that there is no need of continuing the discussion. How well I understand his reluctance, since I have shared it during the major part of my philosophical career![8]

Besides the objections from his students, Donceel feels that the God of our faith, the God revealed by Jesus, can no longer be reconciled with this unrelational God of philosophy:

> Some of the traditional teachings about God seem to contradict what we feel about him in our hearts. The God for whom it makes no difference whatsoever whether there is a

Creation or Incarnation, the God who is totally unaffected by human suffering, does not look like the God of our faith. The God who, by becoming man, is not different at all from what he would have been if he had not become man, does not look like the God of the Bible.[9]

Donceel finds openings to a new approach in Rahner, Teilhard, Whitehead, and especially in the works of Charles Hartshorne, whom we shall be seeing later on. Donceel personally believes, however, that the most fruitful area of all would be in the thought of Hegel.

To my mind, Donceel states the problem very well; he is trying in his own way to work toward a solution. His scholastic background inclines him to lean toward more traditional concepts, but he is not afraid to launch into newer waters:

> As Christians we believe in a God who struggled, who suffered and who died. I am fully aware that the idea of a God who is both eternal and in time, immutable yet changing, absolute and related to all reality, perfectly simple and indefinitely multiple, affected by all events, even by pain and suffering, presents serious philosophical difficulties. He may appeal to our heart, he shocks our intelligence. We may find it easier to love him, but, for the traditional theist, he is certainly more difficult to understand. He is no longer the God of Aristotle or of Aquinas, he looks more like the God of Hegel and of Whitehead.[10]

Father W. Norris Clarke, S.J. is perhaps one of the leading Thomist scholars in America. He, too, is having second thoughts on the immutability of God. In a recent article entitled "A New Look at the Immutability of God," Clarke mentions two thrusts of modern thought which have made him reconsider his position. The new school of process philosophy is one of these factors. The other is the present religious consciousness "with its strong emphasis on the truly personal relation which must exist between a religiously available personal God and finite persons he has created."[11] Clarke considers the challenge from this latter quarter to be the more urgent and serious.

He admits that process philosophers such as Charles Hartshorne "have a legitimate grievance against the way Thomists have handled, or failed to handle, this problem." He attempts to "explore the resources of the Thomistic metaphysical system to see how far it is capable of making place for a God who can enter into truly personal relations with His creatures."[12] These remarks indicate to me an admission that the God of Thomism is not a very personal God, at least not personal enough. Readers interested in one possible Thomistic approach to this problem are referred to this article. Clarke and Donceel are mentioned especially to make Catholic readers more aware that our scholars have recognized the problem and are working, each in his own way, toward greater clarification.

We would be very remiss if we did not also mention in this context a scholar who may not be very familiar to many. Father Walter Stokes, S.J. died rather prematurely in the mid-sixties. He was the foremost Catholic scholar in Whiteheadian studies, and his death undoubtedly has retarded the understanding and assimilation of Whitehead's thought into Catholic theology.

His general goal, it seems, was to be "concerned with new perspectives and emphases that might help make Thomism more meaningful to ourselves and to our contemporaries. In America...it may be especially valuable to consider the particular way that Whitehead might stimulate rethinking and developing Thomism."[13]

Stokes did his doctoral dissertation on Whitehead and contributed a number of significant articles on the relationship between Thomism and Whitehead. Like Donceel and Clarke, he was aware, perhaps before they were, of the problems we are considering:

> ....Now the question is: Can God's love for this world be more adequately expressed than it has been in the traditional

theistic position which holds that God's knowledge and love of this world involves Him in nothing more than a rational relation?[14]

Stokes sought his answer "from [a] new perspective of Augustinian liberty and the analogy of person," the latter doctrine, according to Stokes, being underdeveloped in Thomism. With these two new starting points he believed "it is possible to conceive of God's relation to the world as real without thereby attributing any imperfection to Him."[15]

Stokes' return to Augustine's notion of person is interesting for several reasons. Robert Grant says that the scriptural intuition from John that "God is love" received precious little attention in the thinking of the early Fathers until Augustine:

> As the doctrine of the Trinity was worked out, the conception of God as love played little part in it until we reach Augustine's famous interpretation of God as the one who loves, the Son as the one who is loved, and the Spirit as the love that binds them together. This idea arises in Christian circles rather late.... Christological statements of the second century generally treat Christ not as the expression of God's love but as the 'reason' of God's mind.[16]

This observation should be borne in mind as we proceed. The fleshing out of the biblical intuition that God is love was not a major part of the development of the early centuries as regards the doctrine of God. It surely is one important avenue of exploration toward a passionate God.

Teilhard de Chardin also points to the concept of love as a factor calling for the reevaluation of God's self-sufficiency. The following quotations and comments are taken from Father Christopher Mooney, an acknowledged expert on Teilhard de Chardin.

Mooney states that in Teilhard's thought "mankind is not a matter of indifference to God; its evolutionary development is meant to move toward and in some way contribute to the final Pleroma of Christ. By his own sovereignly free decision, God is no longer 'absolutely' and 'radically' self-sufficient."[17] Mooney offers these thoughts from Teilhard:

> Let us test every barrier, try every path, plumb every depth. *Nihil intentatum*. . . .It is the will of God, who has willed that he should have need of it [the universe].[18]
>
> Why the supreme interest attached to the completion of the mysterious Pleroma in the most positive terms of Scripture? God is completely self-sufficient, and yet the universe brings to him something vitally necessary.[19]

Mooney comments:

> Teilhard felt very strongly about this need of man under which God has freely placed himself out of the abundance of his love.
>
> What Teilhard is denying. . .is not the abstract idea of God's freedom in creation, but the concrete idea that he is personally independent of this present world whose destiny from all eternity was to be created in Christ.[20]

The fleshing out of this trend in Teilhard's thinking could be another fruitful contribution to the question of God's pathos.[21]

From the above the impression may seem to be given that the pathos of God is at present on very shaky ground in Catholic thought. Such an impression is correct! But the Church also believes in doctrinal development. She is constantly in the process of seeking to understand better and better the total mystery of Christ. Each age brings new focuses, new knowledge, new perspectives to the mysteries of our faith. As stated earlier, I am not addressing myself to the relationship between the pathos of God and the teachings of the Councils on immutability. This certainly must be done. But I believe that my book can help to prepare for the resolution of some of those questions because it treats of the problem *before* any of those doctrinal pronouncements were made. We know that there are limits to the reinterpretation of doctrines. But what those limits are in relation to the immutability of God are questions not specifically met here.

The word "horizon" is very much part of the intellectual scene today.[22] Every person has an horizon. This is his vision of reality, together with the language tools and concepts he possesses to think and speak about that reality. Also limited is his view of the problem, and therefore the kinds of questions he asks. One cannot see and perform beyond his horizon.

In reinterpreting doctrines, the best we can do is try to acquire the most accurate picture possible of both past and (our) present horizons. Whatever new and legitimate knowledge an age acquires must somehow be reconciled with that of former ages, now understood in a new light.

What we are involved in means acquiring new perspectives on a core truth which is found primarily in the biblical revelation. But the Spirit inspires each age with new insights into this core truth. The meaning of any doctrine has something to do with seeing it ever anew through the eyes of both past and present, for each age brings out a new facet of the core truth. To exalt the perspective of any one age over that of another, and to say that such and such an age gave the final nuances to such and such a question is to put the truth in an iron cast.

Our journey will take us from the world of the scriptures into the first two centuries A.D. when Greek philosophical notions began to be employed to elaborate the truths of the faith. J. C. Murray says, in his book *The Problem of God*, that there is a natural tendency of the mind to move from "description to definition...from inquiry into the reality of God's presence to inquiry into the reality of the God who is present. The biblical question, whether God is with us, is organically related to the patristic question, what the God-who-is-with-us-is."²³

What this means is that in scripture God is always spoken of in personal and "functional" categories. We know him by what he does for us, by the kinds of relationships he chooses to have. Later on in the history of the Church, the attempt is made to speak of this God in an entirely different mode of thought and expression. In the words of Father Murray:

> "It is the passage from description of a thing-in-its-function-in-regard-to-me to definition of the thing-in-its-subsistence-as-a-thing-in-itself...."²⁴

It was, as we shall see, the passage from Yahweh and Father, to the Existant and the Unknowable.

The general contention of this book is not that such a transition was illegitimate, or even, in a sense, unsuccessful. They did the best they could with the philosophical concepts available to them. The contention is that in some ways the philosophical mode was *substituted* for the biblical mode; also, that it is legitimate (and even necessary) to rethink the question in the light of our own horizon.

For it is commonplace in theology today to state that doctrines are not so much finishing points as bases for further reflection—starting points as well as guidelines and boundaries. It is the task of the Church to speak the message of God's saving love in a way that people of every age can understand. I believe that the present position on the question of God's immutability demands just such a reinterpretation for the people of our time.

It is also my conviction, in agreement with Clarke, Stokes, and others, that the thought of Whitehead and the process philosophers and theologians provides one viable option for Catholic theologians in the task of reformulation of the faith. We will return to Whitehead in the last chapter. But Whitehead must be adapted. No Church Father, no scholastic, ever took over without qualification the philosophical system of any great philosopher. Plato and Aristotle were adapted; Whitehead can be adapted too.

With all the problems facing the modern world, how can anyone spend time writing about the pathos of God! I believe the question has everything to do with the wholeness of mankind, because the question of God has everything to do with it. There is only one real evil: to be isolated, cut off from God. There are many problems in the world which are evil precisely because they add to this separation. Many of them must be solved before a man can even humanly relate to God.

Man's belief in and notion of who God is is vitally connected with his deepest well-being. We are constituted by our relationships. Could we say that at the deepest level man really is how he believes himself related to God? I believe so. And Christianity in general presents a truly sublime picture of man's true worth—a child of the Father, passionately loved by the Son to the point of death. This is indeed the Good News—that we are loved by God in an unimaginable way.

And yet, I say it with reverence, there is a fly in the ointment, there is a doubt in the depths of the soul—an unanswered question, a coldness: God does not change. He created me, he sent his Son to save me, he loves me—but he does not change.

One reason for the "death of God" movement is that the Hellenic god has died. (It is interesting to point out here that while Abraham Heschel would not even pronounce the phrase "death of God" as being too blasphemous, he strove all his life to foster the concept of God's *pathos*.) "The modern experience of nature [means] the beginning of a post-Hellenic age rather than the beginning of a post-christian age. What will not do in our era is not the idea of God as such but the Hellenic idea of God...."[25]

Where did the chilling notion of Ardrey's "presence" come from? I don't know. It isn't the Christian Father who loved us so much that he sent his only Son. But is Ardrey's notion a popular notion? Is the notion of impassibility helping to foster such a concept of God? I can't help believing that it is.

There are many obstacles to a belief in God. Some of these concern our notions of who God is. Many people reject not the true God but some false notion of God. I believe that one aspect of our teaching about God that needs to be rethought is his immutability. No doubt, people with a strong faith are helped by God to work out the problems between his immutability and the meaning of their lives to him. But for those with weak faith, is it possible that this aspect of doctrine is an added burden? Do many believers walk around with this unresolved question in their hearts: Does anything I do really matter to God?

Stop and *think* for a moment. Ask yourself: Does anything I do, enjoy, or suffer, really affect God in any way? (Pause) What is your answer? Most probably, No. If I had asked you to consult your *heart*, you might have been more inclined to say Yes.

Erwin Goodenough, in his remarks on *The Theology of Justin Martyr*, has some insights very apropos to this schizophrenic mentality. He says that when Christianity arrived on the scene, the converts, both Jew and Gentile, simply took over uncritically the notions about God that were then part of Hellenistic Judaism. At the time, there were not many dogmas about God, and no consistent unification of ideas. But this didn't bother ordinary folk:

> For Hellenistic Judaism did not question the legitimacy of its worship by the implications of its theories of the nature of God. *It philosophized about an Absolute, but prayed to God the Father* (Italics mine). Ordinary Greek Jews would have only understood the Jewish God of Abraham, while they would have used the philosophical phrases of the learned with the indiscrimination of unintelligence. Early Greek Christianity had no incentive for going behind this careless mingling

of devotion with philosophical jargon. The devotional personal view of God, helped out by a few mysterious phrases, is all that has ever been needed or desired by the mass of Christians.26

Hellenistic Judaism refers to the thought and culture which arose among Jews living in diaspora situations, for example, in places like Alexandria.

"Philosophized about an Absolute, but prayed to God the Father"! This is God's mercy to us, that most people trust their religious intuitions and don't pay too much attention to all the abstractions about God! I believe that most people believe very deeply that what they do affects God in some real way—they matter to him. They might not *say* or think out loud that their lives affect God, but this is due partly to a poverty of theological and philosophical notions which render the expression of the experience very difficult. At present, our tradition does not afford the language tools to speak about this aspect of our relationship to God and his to us. Another factor, of course, is the present teaching of the Church.

C. H. Dodd, in his book *The Bible and the Greeks*, says that in two early translations of the Hebrew bible into Greek, there was a different rendering of the famous text from Exodus 3:14; and that in the translations of Aquila and Theodotion, Ex. 3:14 was not translated "I am who I am" but rather "I will be who I will be." Dodd says that this use of the future tense was much closer to the meaning of the Hebrew.27 "I am who I am" was the translation in the Septuagint, the first Greek translation, and the bible used most by the Christians. Even though Aquila and Theodotion were reactionary types, and thought that the hellenizing of the ancient faith had gone too far, still, modern studies confirm their choice.

In a significant article on this question, Michel Allard summarizes the work of several prominent biblical scholars on the meaning of Ex. 3:14. After explaining the ins and outs of the Hebrew verb "to be" he also concludes that "the future sense is grammatically more exact. Yahweh is not he who is, but he who will be, and even more particularly still, he who will be with. The least inadequate translation to us seems to be: I will be who I will be."[28]

> This verb *hayah* does not mean 'to be.' It is more nearly understood by the verb 'to become' in English. ...The LXX (Greek) translation of these three Hebrew words...cannot thus be a true representation of this self-revelation of God. God is not...the 'self-existent one' of the philosophers. If we then translate the words by the English phrase 'I become what I become,' we are drawing nearer to its meaning in the original than if we abide by the translation 'I am that I am.'[29]

Davidson, the author of the article "God" in the *Dictionary of the Bible*, has an enlightening comment on this. He also agrees that this verb in the imperfect has the sense of a future. Then he says:

> It seems evident that in the view of the writer 'ehyeh and Yahweh are the same: that God is 'ehyeh, 'I will be,' when speaking of Himself, and Yahweh, 'he will be,' when spoken of by others. What he will be is left unexpressed—He will be with them, helper, strengthener, deliverer.[30]

"I will be who I will be." "I will become who I will become." "I am becoming what I am becoming." "I will be with you." What do these phrases, this name of God mean, as far as our relatedness to God is concerned? Does the name mean this: "As we go on in our life together, I will always be with you and, by helping you, reveal more and more of myself to you. Who I am cannot be captured in one name. As we go on together I will gradually reveal new aspects of who I am. Your only security will be my changing name, how I meet you throughout your history."

Or does it mean this: "I will become *with you* who I will become. My desire is to be intimately joined to the life of my people. Your hopes, joys, sorrows and pains will be mine also. I will be with you in all of them, sharing in all of them, being affected by all of them. What you become will affect me as well, for we are both involved in life together."

Of course, the question of the pathos of God does not rise or fall on the interpretation of Ex. 3:14. But I believe the now common interpretations we have mentioned are part of a larger web and pattern, the whole of which tend in the direction of pathos. If not pathos, then certainly it lends weight to the modern notion that religion and the concepts of religion—including God—evolve. We no longer believe in a God who orders the wholesale destruction of towns and villages, although such a God is in the Old Testament. The God of Jesus—the God revealed in the Person of Jesus—is not compatible with a God of destruction.

And the notion of pathos then? Is it an idea struggling for life in the religious consciousness of man, or is it an aboriginal notion breathing its last? That is the question; that is what this book is about.

PART I: A PAIR OF GLASSES

2. Both Are Words of God

A legend tells posterity that when the Schools of Shammai and Hillel reached the climax of their spiritual controversy, a heavenly voice was heard, saying that both schools proclaimed the words of the living God. . . .Both views of God, the literal and the allegorical, have their rights and places in Judaism. Both are the words of true religion, of the living God.

Marmorstein, *The Old Rabbinic Doctrine of God*

Thinking about God is historical thinking, and that in two senses: the idea of God has a history, and those who think about God think through an historically formed mind. The task of the theologian, is not the attempt to move outside his historicity—such an attempt constitutes a fallacy and not a virtue—but to accept its implications and limitations. Methodologically this means that the theologian must point to the historical perspectives that underlie the idea of God in its development and, in his own constructive thought, must work self-consciously with an historical perspective informed by the psychological and cosmological understanding of his own times.

Burton Z. Cooper, *The Idea of God*

I am aware that many of the questions in these next two chapters are very debatable. What I intend is to offer some insights of modern psychology and the study of languages to serve as eye-glasses for a twentieth-century man to view the development of the idea of God in the early centuries.

When you sit in the optometrist's office to be fitted for new glasses, he keeps flipping various lenses, now in front of this eye, now in front of that, and he keeps asking "Is that better? Is that better? How's that?" Little by little the focus is adjusted and the vision comes in clearer and clearer. Little by little the correct lenses are found for your eyes. Something similar is being attempted in these next two chapters.

Thus, I do not claim that they will necessarily give 20/20 vision! I do claim that the insights of these chapters will help us see *better* the development of the idea of God, and that these glasses can offer some fruitful insights and perspectives into the pathos of God. The doctrine of the pathos of God (if doctrine it becomes) will have to be validated from many different angles.

What a marvelous and incredible piece of God's handiwork is the human brain! It is the most complex, the most intricate organization of matter in the whole universe. It is hundreds of times more specialized than our most advanced computers. In an instant it can recall scenes from many years ago, details of sight and sound which have been stored away in recesses who knows where. With our imagination we can rearrange images and concepts and fashion exciting stories, pictures, new creations of all kinds. But the most marvelous feature of our brain is that *it puts us into contact with God.*

This may seem like a very "rationalistic" approach to God. This is only because many people equate "brain" with "mind," that is "intellect"; and "intellect" is then equated with "reason" and reason with "logic." All this portrays our Western bias towards the word "brain."

It is a fact that every kind of knowing is eventually rooted and located in the brain. The brain is our computer center, our central control tower. Ultimately it is the instrument par excellence through which we have any knowledge of reality.

A fact very closely related to the topic of this book is

that our knowledge of reality is conditioned by our instruments. It can be no other way. A telescope cannot hear sounds, a radio cannot transmit a picture, our ears cannot tell what color is. Also (and this is obvious but often forgotten), our instruments do not apprehend the whole of reality. There are more sounds in the room where you are sitting than you can pick up; there is more light streaming in than you can process. If all the sounds and all the light which were around you came flooding into your little world, they would blow you apart. You would not be able to handle them. We can only see and hear according to our instruments. Like everything else, then, our knowledge of God is also conditioned by the quality of our instruments.

It is a fairly well-established fact now that there are in man two major modes of consciousness or awareness—two fairly distinct ways of apprehending reality. We do not say two ways of thinking because, like the word "brain," "thinking" already connotes to Westerners a particular way of thinking, i.e., rational, logical awareness. For our purposes in this book, we shall describe these two modes as "intuitive" and "rational," although the differences between them are not always so clear. As we go on, I will try to flesh out more precisely the meaning of each of these terms, but, when all is said and done, "intuitive" and "rational" will remain the two best words for describing these two modes of consciousness.

Many years ago the American philosopher William E. Hocking succinctly summed up what I will be trying to say in this chapter, and what modern science is confirming more and more by its findings. He said: "After all, the intellect is not a separate organ of the mind. Both intuition and the intellect are the mind in action: intuition recognizing the presence of objects, intellect defining what they are. They are inseparable. They constitute a working pair.... As intuition is helpless without intellect, it must always be accompanied and followed by conceptual thinking. Intuition is not wisdom; and intellect is not wisdom; wisdom is the union of intuition and intellect."[1]

The Eastern mind, it seems, has not exalted the logical, rational function of the mind to the point of equating the former with the latter. Rather, it speaks of "consciousness," and this consciousness is complex, involving both rational and intuitive (irrational, emotional) aspects. For the Eastern mind, consciousness is not the rational element which attempts to dominate and analyze reality. Rather, it is simply man's total ability to reflect upon and be at one with that reality.[2]

There have been a series of books lately (e.g. Theodore Roszak's *Where the Wasteland Ends*) which have hammered home the proposition that the Western mind is sick because it has exalted the rational aspect of consciousness above and beyond its due and out of all proportion to its importance. A whole civilization is being brought up on the notion that scientific objectivity—the rational mind—is the only avenue to reality. This belief is causing havoc in our society; it is a bad, mad science of knowledge.

I agree basically with this critique. But the ironic thing happening now is that science itself is discovering, *through its own experiments*, that there is another mode of consciousness, another way of apprehending the world which must be taken into consideration in the search for truth. In short, *the rational mind is confirming the existence and the necessity of the intuitive mind*!

To me, this is very exciting. Not that I needed science to tell me that there were irrational processes in me! No. But it is another instance of the truth conquering. For several centuries now the rational, logical, scientific mind of man has cut reality into pieces and made intuition feel inferior and like a second-class citizen in the world of nature. Now, intuition is achieving its proper place.

"Well, you've succumbed after all," I hear the reader saying. "You needed logical, scientific reasoning to give a firm basis to your intuitive powers!" Yes and no. We want to keep our balance. We do not believe in intuition simply because it is scientifically proven. On the other hand, scientific, rational demonstration *is one path* to truth, or, rather, it is the other intertwining thread which, along with intuition, leads to the truth. This is precisely the thesis of this chapter: both of these ways are roads to truth, and consequently both can speak the word of God. In this chapter I would like to present some of these scientific findings.

In relation to the question we are discussing in this book—the pathos of God—we will be talking very much about how people from different cultures and with different backgrounds expressed their understanding of him. The reality of God was understood differently because people have different kinds of eyes and mentalities. Whitehead says that our experiences are the glasses through which we see reality. What we hope becomes clearer is that each of these different ways of seeing God throughout the ages has a place, and each way can tell us something different about him. It is not proper, however, to *substitute* one way for another. The findings in this chapter should be kept in mind, then, when we take our excursion in the chapters to follow.

Science has been discovering that there are basically two distinct modes by which we know the world. First, a few facts from the world of physics.

> The duality of light's behavior arises not from the light 'itself' (if such an idea even has any meaning), but from the observation of light as it interacts with experimental equipment and in the description of such observations in language that only contain the classical terms 'wave' and 'particle' as models of the phenomenon.[3]

To simplify even further. All this means that we do not know what light is "in itself." We only know it as seen under different conditions of observation. I would like to make a few comments on this notion of knowing things "in themselves" because I think it has a great deal to do with the subject of this book.

We do not know anything "in itself," if by that phrase is meant knowing something exhaustively, in its deepest and absolute essence and nature, and in all its aspects. We do not know anything in this way—neither our mothers, nor our friends, nor ourselves, nor flowers, nor the heavens, and certainly not God. We do not walk around relating to things and people "in themselves." *We relate to them as we know and experience them.*

For me, the reality of a rose is not what it is "in itself" but in what I see and experience it is—its color, its fragrance, its setting in a garden. That is what a rose really is to me, and it is the same with everything in the universe. I am curious about learning more about the universe, and of what is yet to be discovered. But what the universe is "in itself" is a non-problem because it can never be known. Much more exciting is what I actually experience of the universe. For me, the universe really is the sun and the moon and the stars and the galaxies and whatever else can be known with the powers God has given us.

The same applies to God. We do not know who God is "in himself." The truest thing for me is not what I *do not* know about God, but what I *do know.* I do not walk around relating to an unknown God, or to God "in himself." I relate to God as Father, Son, and Holy Spirit, to God as revealed by Jesus. God for me is Yahweh and Elohim and El-Shaddai and all the other names by which he has revealed himself. God is what people have experienced him to be, how he related to them, how he manifested himself. This is not *all* he is. But as far as I am concerned, in my day to day life with him, he is much more what he has revealed himself to be than what I do not know about him:

> There is no trace in the Old Testament of the idea that God as revealed to men is not God as He really is in Himself, or that

His revelation of Himself is meant merely to be regulative of human life, while what He is in truth remains far away in a transcendental background out of which it is impossible for it to advance, or into which it is impossible for men to penetrate. *The revelation God gives of Himself is a revelation of Himself as He is in truth, though it may be impossible to reveal Himself fully* to men (italics mine).[4]

If someone wishes to say that the Blessed Trinity is a revelation of what God is "in himself," I would not quibble. But I would agree only in this sense—that the Trinity is the deepest truth we know about God, and these are still human words to express the unexpressible. The contrast I am making is between God as known and unknown. It is not a deeper knowledge of God to relate to him as the Unknowable. It is a *different* way of relating to him. But most of the time I do not relate to the Unknowable, but to the Trinity.

As a result of these and other findings in quantum physics, Niels Bohr, who has been called the "Nestor of atomic physics," has developed what he calls the principle of complementarity. The fact that scientists obtain different results from their observations of the same phenomena should not disturb them. These results should simply be seen as complementary: "Far from restricting our efforts to put questions to nature in the form of experiments, the notion of complementarity simply characterizes the answers we can receive by such inquiry...."[5] A variety of answers does not mean there are *no* answers. It simply means that the answer will not be simple but many-faceted, and that this is the nature of reality as best we can know it.

I am going to link up "Hebrew" with "intuitive" and "Greek" with "rational," although in a real sense this is an oversimplification. I believe, however, that it is close enough to the truth to be a most useful approach.

At the very end of the book on *Hebrew Thought Compared With Greek* (which we shall be using extensively in the next chapter), the author Thorlief Boman has this to say about Niels Bohr's findings:

> Niels Bohr has continually emphasized that the findings of atomic physics are complementary, i.e., they cannot be correctly described without resorting to expressions which are logically irreconcilable. Thus, some experiments show that the atom has wave structure, and others show that it consists of particles (quanta). If both are right, reality possesses opposite properties which complete each other. Bohr calls the unitariness of opposite manifestations of a phenomenon *complementarity*. In that sense, Hebrew and Greek thinking are complementary; the Greeks describe reality as *being*, the Hebrews as *movement*. Reality is, however, both at the same time; this is logically impossible, and yet it is correct.[6]

This passage is like a preview of coming events; presented at this time it may help the reader to see where these findings on the nature of consciousness will eventually lead. All reality—and God too—is apprehended through two distinct kinds of instruments, rational consciousness and intuitive consciousness. The instrument affects the nature of the knowledge, and thus of the object. We cannot separate the object from the instrument, subject from object. This is also one of the basic conclusions of many modern schools of philosophy: we are bound up with what we know. There is no such thing as purely objective knowledge, as knowing reality "in itself."

Psychology and studies on the human brain reinforce and throw more light on these findings in atomic physics. "A growing body of evidence demonstrates that each person has two major modes of consciousness available, one linear and rational, one arational and intuitive."[7] Each hemisphere of the brain seems to deal with one of the predominant modes of consciousness. Each hemisphere has the potential to develop any function, but, normally, the left hemisphere is involved with analytic, logical and linear thinking. It processes information sequentially and specializes in analysis, in taking things apart to examine them. This is most often in the left hemisphere because ninety-five-percent of all people are right-handed, and, as is well known, the left side of the brain controls the right side of the body.

The other, "right" hemisphere operates more holistically. As Hocking put it, it deals with the presence of objects, meets them as a whole unit and does not attempt to cut reality up into pieces. This hemisphere is limited in the use of language. It is orientated in space and time and is involved in artistic endeavors, crafts, body images, and the recognition of faces. Its mode of operation is more relational and simultaneous—spontaneous. It controls the left side of the body. Consequently, we shall speak of the left and right hemispheres, meaning thereby the rational and intuitive aspects of consciousness respectively.

The reader will always bear in mind that these in fact can be reversed in a left-handed person. Our practical hand requires coordination and exactness and attention to specific detail if it is to manage the artifacts of the practical world. The side of the brain which controls this practical series of functions develops rational, analytical thought-patterns. It all depends on the *dominant* side. Even this word "dominant" is a cultural bias. In the West we tend to think of the rational as the dominant side, that is, the side which is most important, most necessary, most useful for life. Depending on the mode of consciousness, each side is dominant. They are simply dominant in different ways.[8]

My contention will be that, in the theology dealing with God's attributes, the kind of knowledge which flows from rational thought has been overemphasized and allowed to be substituted for the kind of knowledge which streams from intuition.

The overemphasis of rational knowledge in the field of science is the thesis of Thomas Blackburn in his article which we have been quoting.

There is a knowledge other than quantitative knowledge, and there are other ways of knowing besides reading the position of a pointer on a scale. The human mind and body process information with staggering sophistication and sensitivity by the direct sensuous experience of their surroundings. We have, in fact, in our very selves, 'instruments' that are capable of confronting and understanding the blooming, buzzing, messy world outside the laboratory.[9]

Blackburn quotes A. N. Whitehead (one of my secular saints) as one of the first people to recognize that scientists have been looking at the world with only one eye.

The goal—in theology, in science, and in every aspect of life—is to have these two modes of consciousness work together, so that we can be enriched by the truth coming to us in each way. Thus, Blackburn drew up a list of guidelines concerning these two modes which I think should apply to the question of knowledge about God as well:

1) the language, the epistemology, and the models of the two approaches all present us with conflicting pictures of reality;
2) which description of nature one gives depends entirely on one's method of knowing;
3) both approaches are 'rational.' That is, both use a consistent logic, based clearly on the observation of the phenomena;
4) it goes without saying that neither approach to nature can be subsumed into the other. A number is not an experience, nor an equation the same thing as intuition. These things are projections of nature into separate (disjunct) mental spaces.
5) sensuous information is not independent of quantitative knowledge, since they both have their referent in the same system of nature. Of course, abuses of both methods are possible. . . .
6) by the same reasoning, both sensuous and quantitative descriptions of nature may be true; they lead, by the

process of continuous self-correction, to reliable models of nature.

7) Finally, neither sensuous nor quantitative knowledge of nature is complete. In fact, it should be clear...that each is really an undernourished view of nature, because each mode lacks information available through the other. Indeed, it is difficult to think of a single problem that has been attacked by both modes of knowing, so different are the mind-sets of the two classes of investigators![10]

Generally speaking, if we could substitute "God" for "nature," "intuitive" for "sensuous," "intellectual" for "quantitative," we would have, I think, some good guidelines to arrive at a knowledge of God, the truths of our faith, and indeed, the whole of life.

The relevance of these guidelines to the knowledge of God is evident. I hope it becomes clearer as we proceed that the biblical intuitions about God's pathos (his jealousy, anger, love, etc.) flow from a different consciousness than the conclusions of abstract reasoning. Both approaches are legitimate. Both approaches are "rational" in the sense that characteristics of God are "deduced" from the vantage point of each particular mode of knowing. When biblical man sins he experiences God's anger and therefore says that God is angry. This is a perfectly "reasonable" conclusion. According to his religious consciousness, God really *is angry*.

The Greek, philosophical mind also believes that sin angers God. But because of his method and because he goes on to ask different questions, he concludes that God cannot *really* be angry; his reason tells him that God cannot change.

To repeat: my contention will be that neither of these approaches to the knowledge of God can be subsumed into the other. Somehow they are both true, both avenues to God, both capable of discovering truths about him. Many dangers lurk in the exclusive use of only one.

Intuition is capable of seeing anything—and has. Likewise reason, beginning from the wrong premises can reason to almost anything—and has. (I speak in reference to God.) But working together, using the agreed upon truths about God that have deeply nourished man down through the ages, these two avenues can lead us to a balanced knowledge of God. As Blackburn says, "If one asks 'What is color?' the complete answer to such a question can be found only in the complementary descriptions from physics and art."[11] Similarly, it will be argued, if one asks "Who is God?" the answer can only come from complementary descriptions from intuition and reason.

3. Ezekiel and Aristotle

Once when many wise men were gathered about his board, the rabbi of Rizhyn asked: 'Why are the people so set against our master Moses ben Maimon?' A rabbi answered: 'Because in a certain passage he asserts that Aristotle knew more about the spheres of heaven than Ezekiel. So why should we not be set against him?'

The rabbi of Rizhyn said: 'It is just as our master Moses ben Maimon says. Two people entered the palace of a king. One took a long time over each room, examined the gorgeous stuffs and treasures with the eyes of an expert and could not see enough. The other walked through the halls and knew nothing but this: 'This is the king's house, this is the king's house. A few more steps and I shall behold my Lord, the King.'

Martin Buber, *Tales of the Hasidim*

Since both our chief senses, sight and hearing, must pay for their accomplishments the price of an externally stamped bias, both highly developed peoples of ancient times, Hellas and Israel, could achieve their magnificent contributions to civilization only in virtue of their bias. As their cultural successors and heirs, we can pay them no greater homage than to attend equally to both heritages, to protect them, and, if possible, to find a synthesis between them just as we try in our own lives to make the most of all five senses if we would understand reality and have a thorough grasp of all of it.

Thorleif Boman,
Hebrew Thought Compared With Greek

The sin, the fault of theology and piety, is to succumb to the temptation of interpreting *dabar* in terms of reason or of an idea which Greek paganism gives to it. Then man replaces the word which God addresses to him by his own words about God, about a God which man has created by his own fantasy.

Wilhelm Vischer,
"The Holy Language, Source of Theology"

Especially for someone interested in process thought (as I am), Thorleif Boman's book which I have been quoting makes for truly exciting reading. As we shall see, at almost every turn he concludes that the Hebrews had an all-pervading *process view* of reality. If his view is accepted in the academic world, then some very interesting questions emerge which bear directly on our present subject.

It is a fact, a curious fact, that the Gospels were only preserved in the Greek language. On the other hand, if we recall that the hellenization process had already been going on for three hundred years, it is perhaps not so curious after all. Still, one would have thought that the Jewish Christians would have appreciated having the Gospels put into Hebrew, or at least leaving some of the Aramaic originals around.

Be that as it may, the early Jewish Christians were evidently satisfied that the realities of their faith were adequately translated into the Greek language. After all, it was a common sense thing to do: make the Good News available to the wider audience of the Hellenistic world. Many of the writers were no doubt more Greek than Hebrew. The question being broached here concerns the translation of Hebrew concepts into Greek words.

No doubt Jewish Christians with their semitic background "read into" the Greek words many elements which a non-Jew would not see. Also, the Jewish Christians would have "read out of" the Greek words whatever notions clashed with their ancient faith. But what about the non-Jews? The question may be asked as to how much of the Hebrew connotations and deep religious meaning was missed by those non-Jews who read the Greek words with Greek eyes. They were people like Justin and the apologists (whom we shall see later), and all the other people among the gentiles converted to Christianity. What did *Theos* mean to those who never knew Yahweh? I think it accurate to say that such people would be relating to a slightly different God, since the words used to describe him were colored by the mentality of the cultural climate and spirit.

In this chapter we are going to take a look at the characteristics of Greek and Hebrew thought-patterns as a preparation to answering some of these questions. Generally we shall conclude that Hebrew thinking approximates more the features of the right (intuitive) hemisphere, and Greek the left (rational) hemisphere. The lines, of course, are not a hundred-percent clear. As already mentioned, there is a "logic" to intuition as much as to reason. But since the Hebrews were a sensuous, outdoor, explosive people, their window to reality was predominated by intuitive elements. The Greeks, on the other hand, were urban, restrained, and sophisticated: "If Israelite thinking is to be characterized, it is obvious first to call it dynamic, vigorous, passionate, and sometimes quite explosive in kind; correspondingly, Greek thinking is static, peaceful, moderate, and harmonious in kind."[1] Let us then look more closely at the characteristics of these two mentalities which have played such a large part in fashioning the consciousness of the Western world.

The basic meaning of Israelite verbs is to express a movement or an activity. Things standing still are seen as the end of a movement carried through to a standstill; repose is the end of a movement, or else contains a latent movement. "Our analysis of the Hebrew verbs that express standing, sitting, lying, etc., teaches us that motionless and fixed being is for the Hebrew a nonentity; it does not exist for them. Only 'being' which stands in inner relation with something active and moving is a reality to them. This could also be expressed: only movement (motion) has reality."[2]

Verbs showing conditions or properties designate first of all the *becoming* of the conditions and qualities in question.

The verb "to be" is of special interest to us because of the characteristics it gives to God's being (Ex. 3:14).

The Hebrew verb "to be" has three basic meanings: it can signify 1) real becoming, 2) the becoming of inner being, or 3) becoming something new by vocation. Whence did the Hebrews obtain their basic notion of "being"? Its source is psychological: "It is correct to say in the case of the Hebrews that 'being'. . .represents an inner activity which is best to be grasped by means of psychological analogies with human psychic life; with that we come to the heart of the matter. In the full Old Testament sense 'being' is preeminently *personal being.*"[3]

This is an extremely important statement for us. What model is to be the basis for our speaking about reality, and consequently about God? Such models can only come from our experience. The Greeks and Hebrews both gave God the characteristics of their experience, but the Greeks clothed him with the qualities of the rational hemisphere, while the Hebrews clothed him with the qualities of the intuitive hemisphere.

The fact that the Hebrews expressed reality according to the features of psychic life is a point of agreement with the process philosophers; also, in the next chapter, we shall see that personality is the basic intuition about God in the Old Testament. Whitehead's argument is that the reality we know best is our own interior experience; this is what we *really know* if we know anything. Therefore, he makes all of reality, including God, in some way univocal to this experience. If we cannot assert this, then we cannot know reality very deeply or accurately. We must take our experience as a piece of all experience—even God's—and proceed to work out the principles that govern all of reality.

Walter Stokes agrees that this is the main issue between Whitehead and much of classical philosophy.

"The crucial issue [between Whitehead and Thomas] is whether or not human experience is the measure of reality. Whitehead's view that all reality must be on a univocal plane with human experience clashes directly with the Thomistic doctrines of the analogy of being."[4]

All throughout this discussion, if we keep in mind that the Hebrews think psychologically, whereas we tend to start from the object, the seeming contradiction in their thinking will be better understood.

Boman limits his discussion of Greek thought to Plato, since it was Platonic thought which predominantly influenced the early Christian Fathers. (In the second century, with which we will be concerned, it was known as the school of Middle Platonism.) What follows would apply to the basic Platonic world view, and we shall go into it in more detail in Chapter 7.

Basically, Plato has two levels of being—the sensible world, and the spiritual, intelligible world. The former, made up of men, animals, plants, and minerals—the things we see—belongs to the kingdom of becoming. Everything on this level is mutable and transitory, "being born and passing away." In the higher, intelligible world, the world of true being, nothing ever changes. There is no coming into being, and no passing away. There is only rest, unalterableness, indestructibility.

The Hebrews, on the contrary, took this world very seriously—and it was very real to them. It was the notion of another, ideal world, someplace, which would have been the less real.

The meaning of the word "word" in these two cultures is another key for understanding how their two basically divergent views of reality can be characterized.

The Hebrew word for "word" (*dabhar*) had little to do originally with the mere spoken word. It was a symbol to give expression to the experience of the basic creative thrust behind all things which pushes things into being. God's *dabhar* is an action which terminates and eventuates in the cosmos. This is why the word expresses a unity of word and deed, and can mean both. Now, to us, this would be a contradiction: a word is one thing, an action another. But *dabhar* stands for the creative *push* at work, the force which drives all things before it. It is thus an effective force. "My word will not return empty to my mouth." If there is no unity between an action and the speech which produced it, the word is no word at all; it is a lie, a lying word. In English, a lie can also be a word. But for the Hebrew, if the "word" was not true to the speaker, it would be no word at all.

Also, in the *dabhar* of Jahweh, the word has a special revelatory nature: "*Dabhar* is more than an emanation, or a hypostasis of the divinity; *dabhar* is a manifestation of Jahweh, and indeed the highest form of that manifestation. *Dabhar* is Jahweh as he is recognizable to mortal man."[6]

"*Dabhar* is Jahweh as he is recognizable to mortal man." This is a point close to the heart of our discussion. The very point at issue concerning the pathos of God is how to interpret the word of God to man in the scriptures. Is this word like a mask on an actor's face, with the *real* face behind it—the mask and the face being two, quite different things? Or, is it more like sunlight coming to us through various refractions? What finally hits our eyes is *really the sunlight*, only now adapted to our vision. But the light is not a mask for something else.

Is the word of God a mask, or a beam of light? The beam of light is more the meaning of the Hebrew view of reality; the mask is closer to the Greek, as we shall now see.

As the root notion behind *dabhar* was "that which effects or pushes forward," the Greek word for "word" (*logos*) "comes from a root word which means to gather, but to gather to put together in order, and thus to *arrange*."[7] It later took on the sense of "meaning, the ordered and reasonable content" of things.

The Greeks were very interested in the question, "What is the thing *really*, that thing over there separate from me? What is its essence and nature?" When they discovered this meaning, this nature, they called it the *logos* of the thing, that thing's meaning.

What is its ultimate and deepest *logos*, meaning? According to Plato, its ultimate meaning is in the world of changeless ideas. Those eternal, unchanging ideas are the truly real, and all things on earth are merely shadows of those intellectual realities. Earthly realities are like masks.

In this view there is much more of a disjunction between the material thing and the "real" world, the world of ideas. Thus, the two words, *dabhar* and *logos* "teach us what the two peoples considered primary and essential in mental life: on the one side the dynamic, masterful, energetic—on the other side the ordered, moderate, thought out, calculated, meaningful, rational."[8]

The question of anthropomorphisms in the bible is of particular interest to us, and we will be considering it in more detail in the next chapter. Everyone is familiar with the fact that human titles were applied to God—king, father, Lord—as well as parts of the body (anthropomorphisms properly so called) and human emotions and affections (anthropopathisms). *The* question as far as our pathos of God topic is concerned is: how are we to interpret these expressions? We know that God does not have a hand like ours, nor walk around on two legs. But when the bible says that he repents, is jealous, is angry, how are these images from human emotions to be explained?

The answer hinges on many things, but one of them is whether you are a Hebrew or a Greek. In the Hebrew view of reality the image really shares in the reality it expresses:

> Since these bodily parts and bodily phenomena are images of qualities, the descriptions of Jahweh's appearance is, really, a description of his essence, of his spiritual personality as it is

accessible to men, thus a description of his 'name.' Since the poet (Isaiah 30:27-30) calls the theophany Jahweh's *shem* (appearance), he has given us the key to the correct understanding of the anthropomorphisms: Jahweh's *shem* is the sum total of his qualities and activity. When men see God's acts, they see in them God so far as he is knowable to men, his essence and qualities. The name is thus a manifestation of divinity.[9]

It will be helpful for our readers to quote this passage from Isaiah, paying attention to the revelation of the name:

> See, the *name* of Yahweh comes from afar,
> blazing is his anger, heavy his exaction.
> His lips brim with fury,
> his tongue is like a devouring fire.
> His breath is like a river in spate
> coming up to the neck.
> He comes to sift the nations with the sieve of destruction,
> to put the bit of his bridle between the jaws of the nations.

My contention would be that this experience of the anger of God really is a sharing in the anger of God. It is refracted through the prism of man's faculties and powers —adapted to his instruments, as it were—but it is not a mask for something else. We really do see the light from the sun, and the Hebrew intuition was that they really did experience the anger of God (as well as his love, compassion, etc.) The image shares in the reality; the *shem* is a sharing in the essence.

It might be objected that anthropomorphisms— expressions which use parts of the body in reference to God—would be simply older and more "primitive" descriptions. The opposite is true. What is perhaps the oldest poem in the Old Testament, the Song of Deborah, mentions no bodily parts at all, and earlier prophets such as Amos and Hosea are much more restrained than the later Deutero-Isaiah in such matters. Earlier accounts employ anthropomorphic divine *actions*, while later documents more often employ *visible* manifestations. One comparison may help.

In Hosea (721) we read: "I myself taught Ephraim to walk, I took them in my arms; yet they have not understood that I was the one looking after them. I led them with reins of kindness, with leading strings of love" (11:3-4). In Ezekiel (539) we read: "The glory of Yahweh came out from the Temple threshold and paused over the cherubs. . . .The cherubs spread their wings and rose from the ground to leave. . .and the glory of the God of Israel hovered over them" (10:18-19). These descriptions are essentially the same since they both serve the same purpose, i.e., they reveal Yahweh's qualities and his being.

The gradual loss of anthropomorphisms was not necessarily an advance on the knowledge of God. This is Boman's opinion:

> Later generations, having failed to grasp the profound meaning of the "anthropomorphisms,' have taken umbrage at their mere humanness, and have preferred more neutral means of revelation like word, spirit, and wisdom. The 'anthropomorphisms,' because of their descriptive power, continue to stand as peerless expressions of the divine being.[10]

There are two more dimensions to this problem which can throw light on our subject.

The Old Testament has a variety of ways to speak of the manifestations of God. Boman says that the Old Testament did form and come up with a very precise theological expression for the appearance or the manifestation of God. It was the *image-of-God* description of man in P's account of creation (1:26). "This *imago Dei* conception is no secondary and peripheral detail, but it is a zenith in Old Testament theology and anthropology."[11]

David Cairns, in his study *The Image of God In Man*, likewise draws attention to the great importance of this expression:

Thus here in 'P,' and here alone, does the Old Testament rise to the formation of a special concept to mark man's otherness from the rest of the world, and his kinship with God. . . .This is the only doctrine of the image which is found *by name* in the Old Testament.[12]

Cairns wrote a book on the meaning of this phrase in the scriptures and throughout the whole of Christian tradition. Here, we wish to reflect on it in the context of our topic. It will be an attempt to distinguish between the Hebrew and the Greek notion of "image." Both views wish to say that God is an active personality. But as far as how God acts and what is the relationship between his manifestations and the world, they differ because of the bias in the different way of knowing.

The most important sense for the Hebrew in the experience of truth was his hearing. They might be called "people of the ears." Hearing for the Hebrew means not only sounds but "listening" to the sensations which pour in from all sides—words, warmth, odors, flavors, and so on. These sensations give to the Hebrew conceptions their characteristics of vibrancy and dynamism; in short, their explosive qualities. And this is why, too, they spoke most of all of God's *word* to them. A nomadic, desert people, they were attuned to the sounds of the world. Their existence depended on their hearing, on their alertness to the sounds of danger and safety around them. (In one sense, hearing seems to be a more comprehensive sense. Helen Keller was once asked which of her senses she would choose to have restored. Without hesitation she said her hearing.)

The Greeks, on the other hand, could be characterized, as Boman says, as "people of the eyes." With their eyes they searched for the essence of things, and the *logos* became the eye of the mind. With their bodily eyes they carved their beautiful statues and molded their breathtaking columns. They wanted to know truth "objectively," the truth as it was in itself, not bound up with sensations or with their own psyches. They wanted to sit still and contemplate reality from the outside, as it were.

Psychologists tell us that the impressions we obtain from our eyes are similar to those of a camera. They are still-pictures, even though we have the impression that the scene is flowing. These sight impressions have the characteristics of form, objectivity and immutability. These are the characteristics of thought, the logical processes of the left hemisphere. They flow from the bias of making truth mostly a matter of sight and consequently of thought.

We Westerners think mostly like the Greeks, so we can perhaps appreciate better their view of reality. These two ways are symbolized by two figures, the thinking Socrates, and a praying Jew:

> When Socrates was seized by a problem, he remained immobile for an interminable period of time in deep thought; when Holy Scripture is read aloud in the synagogue, the Orthodox Jew moves his whole body ceaselessly in deep devotion and adoration. The Greek most acutely experiences the world and existence while he stands and reflects, but the Israelite reaches his zenith in ceaseless movement. Rest, harmony, and self-control—this is the Greek way; movement, life, deep emotion, and power—this is the Hebrew way.[13]

Granted now that there are these two ways of knowing, and that each believes there is a Power who is using the world as a means for action and self-disclosure, what does the phrase "image of God" mean to each?

The word used for "image" in Genesis 1:26 means "the complete likeness of a picture or a statue to the original." Boman also says that image in the ancient world meant not only a copy but "it can also mean a 'radiating, a becoming visible and manifest of the essence in such a way as to have a share in the very substance of the thing itself.'"[14] Thus *eikon* means, in plain words, the coming into appearance of the kernel, the essence of a thing; *it participates in the reality of what it images.* A sign of any kind for the Israelite is an expression of the divine will and power.

What is an eikon to the Greek? The Greek believes that the ultimately real is in another realm altogether, and that the ultimately real are intelligible objects. What he attempts to do is to have in his mind a reflection of that ideal form. Any earthly symbol or eikon, therefore, *because it is changing, mutable, and transitory*, cannot really share in the eternal reality in the same way it can for the Hebrew. For the Greek it can only be a *mere image*, a bridge, a mask. Changeable reality cannot share in immutable reality, the truly real.

Boman says that the phrase "image of God" in Genesis "does not say how God looks in himself but only how he appears before men and is known by them."[15] This is in keeping with the kind of knowledge we find in the Scriptures. It is a functional, relational knowledge, knowledge of God-in-relation-to-man and not God-as-he-is-in-himself.

To repeat (as it is so crucial for the pathos of God), what things are *in themselves* is a non-question because it is impossible to answer. In one real sense, *God is how he appears to us.* Not that this exhausts his Divinity, but his appearance is the best way we can know him.

It seems to me that there are several approaches here: 1) we cannot know God in himself, therefore he is unknowable; this is agnosticism; 2) we can know something about God through his manifestations and appearances, just as we know everything else. And here there are two approaches: a) the Hebrew way; God shares in the appearance, or rather, the appearance reveals the kernel of God, or b) the Greek way: God's appearances are mere copies of what and who he is; we arrive at his truer characteristics through reason and logic. My contention would be that we know God through a combination of the Greek *and* Hebrew ways.

In this book I do not examine the implications of the Incarnation and its bearing on the pathos of God. Something will be mentioned in the last chapter on the necessity for this to be done. But I would like to use the Incarnation to sum up this chapter.

St. Paul says that Christ is designated as the "eikon of the invisible God" (Col. 1:15). Boman says: "The expression is best to be explained in a Hebraic way and means that Christ is the aggregate of the qualities of the invisible God. However, it can also be interpreted in a Greek way and then means that Christ is the becoming visible on earth of the invisible God. The sense remains the same although, as regards form, the interpretations are opposite."[16]

It seems to me that the question of the pathos of God has a great deal to do with the way Jesus is interpreted to be God's *eikon*. In each conception Christ is the image of the invisible God; each can say that Jesus is God. But to how much of Jesus' human nature does the image extend? Does it mean that even the qualities (passions, emotions) of Jesus' human nature are also in God, so that these too are part of the kernel? Or, do we arrive, by some other process (reason and logic) to a notion of the invisible God who is *behind* the appearance of Christ? I think it will become evident, in the chapters that follow, that in regard to the pathos of God, tradition chose the latter route.

PART II: THE JOURNEY

4. Yahweh

It is true that the idea of 'God' first reaches vivid consciousness in an emotional and practical, not in an explicitly logical or analytic form and that this preanalytic form is not particularly simple. There is a wealth of expressions, often highly poetic, not wholly consistent, of feelings, and imperatives of behavior, with a relative absence of definition, analysis, or demonstration. But the dearth of logical technique is partly compensated for by a richness of insight into the fundamental experiences from which alone a meaningful idea of God can be derived. If nothing is sharply defined in primitive theism, neither perhaps is anything wholly or sharply excluded. . . .The Old Testament, the Hymns of Ikhnaton, and the Upanishads are examples of this primitive theism.

> Charles Hartshorne and William Reese,
> *Philosophers Speak About God*

The Biblical idea of God is religious, not philosophical, and as such is, especially in the Old Testament, frankly anthropomorphic. Hence God is represented as both passive and mutable.

> Robert Franks, *Encyclopedia of Religion and Ethics*

The biblical notion of God, had it been taken more seriously, would have prevented theologians from presenting God as an impassive and self-enclosed Being.

> Avery Dulles, *The Survival of Dogma*

This brings us to what strictly constitutes the biblical revelation of God—the knowledge of the customs of the living

God through His acts in the history of salvation. What thus appears to us as God is quite different from what religion or philosophy tell us about Him, and even seems sometimes to contradict it. It is thus that the reading of the Bible, insofar as it describes the works of God, is the source of revelation and the starting-point of faith.

Jean Danielou, *God and the Ways of Knowing*

These facts about intuitive and rational, Greek and Hebrew modes of thought are part of modern man's horizon and vision. Certainly the ancients also knew that there were different ways of seeing reality. Undoubtedly, the Hebrew rabbis in Palestine were aware that their view of the world and of God was different from that of Plato and Aristotle; Clement of Alexandria must have known that his thinking differed from that of Isaiah and Rabbi Akiba. But how much insight did these people have into these differences? How aware were they of the characteristics of each way, of the assets and liabilities? Who can say? We see these modes of thought a little more clearly today; hence we should be able to assess a little better what happened to the notion of God as it passed through their minds and cultures. We should also be able to form a better judgment as to the success of the outcome.

What God is like the God of Israel! Was there ever a God among all the peoples of the earth that loves with the passion and jealousy and tenderness of Yahweh! He is a God who loves enough to chastise and get angry and even to feel regret that he had created man. "Outrageous ideas!" some will say. Yahweh would answer: "Am *I* outrageous? Is it not rather *you* who are outrageous?" What people among all the peoples of the earth have been so blessed? Why should God not get angry, rant and rave like a love-sick husband over the infidelities of his wife? This God was such a scandal to Marcion in the second century that he had to posit two gods: an evil one and a good one. We are all Marcionites at heart; our love is not strong enough to get angry!

No abstraction, this God! No tranquil, lifeless Idea thinking itself in some far-off, isolated splendor. He is an involved God, a concerned God. He travels wherever his people go. He guides them with his constant presence. He protects them from their enemies and chastises them when they are unfaithful to his love. He desires nothing more than to dwell among them, to be at home with them. He gives them laws to guide their actions, makes a covenant with them to express his desires for union. Indeed, in all the earth, what nation has a God such as this!

Who is this God really? To the Hebrew, he is whatever he has revealed his *shem*, his name to be. He really is how he acts toward his people. He is known by what he does. "He is Yahweh, the God of Israel, known for what He is by what He does. He is the unseen partner in Israel's fortunes, afflicted in all their afflictions. Their interests are His, and His ought to be theirs."[1]

At the very beginning of his treatment of "God" in the Old Testament, Eichrodt says: "If the saying *nomina sunt realia* [names are the reality] is valid in any context, it is surely that of the divine name in the ancient world."[2] This applies to Israel par excellence. The names given to God in the Old Testament are keys to an understanding of Israel's conception of the divine nature.

> Indeed, the proclamation of the divine Name is so inseparably connected with the revelation of God himself, that different epochs can actually be distinguished by the mere fact of their using different names for God.... For by revealing his Name God has, as it were, made himself over to them; he had opened to them a part of his very being and given them a means of access to himself.[3]

It is not specifically to our purpose here to enumerate and describe all the names of God in the Old Testament; the reader is referred to the many excellent studies on this.

Our concern is to emphasize the significance of these names in the light of the interpretations of the last two chapters, and especially their significance for the pathos of God. For the names are the reality, the name is the kernel of the essence, the name is the beam of light which we see, not a mask which hides another face. Our goal in this chapter is to develop some of the characteristics of God which apply to *all names*, and to indicate how they point to the notion of pathos.

We saw earlier, in the remarks of Vann, Donceel, Clarke, Hartshorne, and others, that one of the factors calling for a reevaluation of God's immutability is the heightened modern appreciation of the reality and exigencies of personhood. All the psychological disciplines of the last few decades, and many of the philosophies as well, make the notion of an "unrelated person" an impossible concept to accept. Further, we saw in Donceel's remarks that a large number of people in the Catholic tradition still hold for a one-way relationship with God: We are related to God, but God is not related to us. In this view, if there were such a real relationship on God's part, it would demand some kind of change in him.

It may seem like beating the obvious, but we are going to spend a little time here emphasizing the fact that the deepest and most primary intuition about God in the Bible is that he is a *Person*. Do we really need to spend time on this? Does anyone deny it or question it? It is one of the contentions of this book that at one level of our doctrine of God we *do* deny it.

I believe that in the realm of heavy philosophy and theology, it is denied by the doctrine of immutability. How can an immutable Person make a covenant, get angry and jealous? I believe that every teaching about God must conform to the intuition of his personhood. It will not be out of place then to emphasize in the strongest possible terms the personality of God.

In his marvelous book, *The Impassibility of God*

(which surveys the history of Christian thought on the matter, and which I wish someone would reprint!), J. K. Mozley has a short section on the Old and New Testaments. He states that there are two obvious facts about the Hebrew notion of God. First, it always involves a transcendental element, and secondly, there is hardly anything we can call metaphysical speculation. He writes:

> What we need to attend to...is the picture of a mental and emotional life which is common to the prophets as well as to the earlier documents. We are in the presence here of no such metaphysical immutability as belongs, for instance, to Aristotle's notion of God. Love, joy, anger, jealousy, 'repentance,' are all ascribed to God, differing from corresponding feelings in men only by their conformity with God's perfect righteousness
>
> ....
>
> The Old Testament does not give us any sharply defined conception of God: it does not set out to teach either religious philosophy or dogmatics. It bears witness to Him only in the language of faith. This remarkable unsystematic speaking about God...indicates that the living Being of God is a fundamental idea in the Hebrew conception of God. That God is alive rests essentially on the fact that God is a Person.[4]

The nature of God which appears from the total Old Testament witness is a wealth of tensions, a richness of attitudes and responses which flow from the phenomenon of personhood. Why are we such mysteries to ourselves and to others if not because we are persons, deep pools of many tensions, desires, attitudes, etc. No logic can catalogue the reality of person, neither in us nor in God.

The concept of *covenant* demands both a personal and a relational God:

> One does not make a covenant with an idea, nor do we enter upon a relationship with an abstraction. But in the presence of a person, man can bind himself and receive in exchange a promise. It is because God is a living person that he can be

considered as transacting an alliance with humanity or with his people.⁵

The more the covenant is taken seriously as the revelation of God, the more profoundly one can understand the historicity of God and history in God. If God has opened his heart in the covenant with his people, he is injured by disobedience and suffers in the people. What the Old Testament terms the *wrath of God* does not belong to the category of the anthropomorphic transference of lower human emotions to God, but in the category of the divine *pathos*. It is sorrow which goes through his open heart. He suffers in his passion for his people.⁶

The very heart, therefore, of the biblical revelation about the nature of God is that he is Someone—not that he is Being, or Perfection, or Spirit, or Unknowable, or Impassible. He is a living Person, and every other attribute or characteristic or aspect of God must conform to the notion of such a living Person:

In the Old Testament conception of God, nothing stood out from the first so strongly and unmistakably as the *personality* of the God of Israel. There is nowhere even the slightest inclination to the thought of a God without consciousness or will. In the covenant, God acts as a Person with other persons. In short, the God of the old covenant is thoroughly self-conscious, independent of the world, free, personal.⁷

We hope the point has been established: God is a Person. This insight flows from Israel's response to the "interior overmastering of the human spirit by God's personal invasion" (Eichrodt). We consider Israel's response as divinely revealed knowledge about God. Thus we must take with absolute seriousness the personality of God when considering the question of God's pathos.

Unconsciously, the immutability of God is rooted, for many people, in the notion that God is a Spirit. And then, somewhere deep in our religious consciousness, lurks the notion that spiritual beings cannot change. (In our theology we apply this certainly to God, to angels [which is why they cannot repent], and to man after death.) It is an accepted notion that what is spiritual cannot change, God being the chief exemplification of this.

Let it be noted that, in the Old Testament at least, the concept of the "spirituality" of God does *not* appear:

> An unprejudiced evaluation of the Old Testament's humanizing of the deity leads us to see...that in fact it is not the spiritual nature of God which is the foundation of Old Testament faith. It is his personhood—a personhood which is fully alive, and a life which is fully personal, and which is involuntarily thought of in terms of the human personality. It is not the spirituality of God...that forms the basis of the Old Testament belief in God, but His full living personality.[8]

Not even in the prophets do we find a doctrine of divine spirituality. The Spirit of God is spoken of, but this refers to God's inner life much in the same way that man's inner life is spoken of as spiritual. The Spirit of God is conceived, like the spirit of man, as more or less material. It is seen as a wise limitation on God's part that "he should have presented himself and caused himself to be understood primarily as personal, while leaving veiled, so to speak, the fact that he was also spiritual."[9]

The writers of the Bible did not see too much of a danger in leaving the spiritual nature of God somewhat obscure. Before all else they were concerned to safeguard his *personhood.* If that was safeguarded, everything was safeguarded. Recent scholarship rejects the view that the language about God in the Old Testament needs some kind of more "spiritual" and less naive interpretation:

> Those whose task it was to proclaim the divine will regarded it as far less damaging that men should have to grope in the dark on the subject of Yahweh's spiritual nature, than that they should remain unconscious of the personal quality of his

behaviour and operations. A doctrine of God as spirit in the philosophical sense will be sought in vain in the pages of the Old Testament. Not until John 4:24 is it possible to declare: 'God is spirit.'[10]

According to the Bible, there is nothing more fundamental that can be said about God than that he is a living person.

Such stress on the personality of God was marshalled to emphasize in the strongest possible terms that no "attribute" of God, deduced by whatever means, can be contrary to his personhood; nor can he come out less a person than we are. Every age will have slightly different notions of personality, and this is to be expected. But how often, even in our daily lives, we do not give God credit for having as much kindness, consideration, etc., as we have with one another! An "impassible person" may be partly to blame for this tendency.

For our present purposes there is another aspect of God which was also of primary importance in the consciousness of God's people: the God of the Hebrews always remained superior to man, distinct and infinitely superior. He is never "humanized" to the point where man loses respect for him (as in the case of the immoral actions attributed to the pagan gods). In other words, the anthropomorphisms of the Bible are never *exactly* anthropomorphisms. The Eternal is never entirely assimilated to man. There is always a barrier between God and man in the Bible, "a barrier which did not exist on the Greek Olympus or in the Babylonian Pantheon: this is the barrier of sanctity."[11] This sanctity is an aspect of Yahweh's transcendence and basically means two things: that Yahweh is not created, and that he does not sin.

"On the moral plane, the sanctity of Yahweh is absolute: he does not participate in the shameful vices and passions of humanity."[12] The feelings of jealousy, anger, vengeance, and hate attributed to Yahweh are not like those of the pagan gods, or like man's for that matter.

There is always in them a superior moral motif. These passions are related to the infidelity of his people which justifies his outrage and his bursts of anger. These are the expressions of his sanctity, because they are prompted by concern to safeguard his sovereignty, his justice and his honor. God is irritated at the sins of men and chastises them with severity.

> In themselves the notions of anger, jealousy, and hate are not immoral. When anger is caused by the sight of the corruptions of the world...can we say that such sentiments are incompatible with the sanctity of God? Every anthropological notion is obliged to have recourse to these expressions which illustrate better than any abstraction the living and personal character of God. The moral rigorism of the prophets did not consider these sometimes striking expressions as too shocking to use. The O.T. presents God as animated by noble passions, not vicious or base ones.[13]

The prophets of Israel stand at a high-water mark in the religious consciousness of mankind. Rarely have men spoke in such vibrant and powerful words and images of both the tenderness and the indignation of Yahweh. They raged against abuses for God's sake as few men have ever done before or since. They were not concerned with maintaining neat, logical distinctions about God's nature. They were raging with the passion of God himself. They were concerned with *his* rights and with little else!

Along with the notion that God was a person, an equally basic intuition was that he was *jealous*.[14] Thus, the true character of God which the prophets try to protect is this: that God, in his moral dealings, is vastly superior to man's moral dealings and notions. They protest against whatever tends to obscure his personhood, his rights, or his superior moral character.

All this can be accomplished by using anthropomorphisms. It is not anthropomorphisms which they see as a problem. They do not seem too particularly concerned if people conceive of God in a human fashion. "The spiritual and physical realms are not for them [prophets] exclusive antinomies; and for this reason they go on presenting the transphysical in physically conceivable forms as the old sages had done."15

On the other hand, when men tend to humanize God in the *wrong* way, i.e., by seeing his moral attributes *as being just like man's*, then the prophets protest also.

Here is where the phrases which speak of God as "not being like a man" fit in. (These phrases are often used as biblical "proofs" for God's immutability.) As mentioned, the prophets do not get upset if people think of God as affected by the passions of love and anger. They only get upset when men try to color Yahweh with their own baser notions of these ideas, or with downright immoral attitudes of behavior.

Thus, the "God is not a man" phrase in Numbers 23:29, Samuel 15:29, and elsewhere, in their contexts, refer to God's *moral* characteristics: God's moral characteristics are not like man's. "God is no man *that he should lie*," is the complete quote from Numbers. Likewise in Samuel, the same idea: "The glory of Israel will not lie or go back on his word, *for he is not a man to go back on his word*." A reference in Hosea has to do with God not being capricious in his judgments: "I will not give rein to my fierce anger, I will not destroy Ephraim again, for I am God, not man" (11:9).

Such phrases cannot be used to prove what they were never meant to prove. They refer primarily to Yahweh's moral superiority, which is one of the things to be safeguarded against all distortion. The "I am not a man" phrases are not metaphysical statements to prove God's immutability!

Too often have statements such as this been transposed into the metaphysical realm. We saw that something like that happened when Ex. 3:14 was translated into Greek. The Septuagint turned a statement meaning "I will be with you to help you" into a metaphysical statement about God's being, "I am who am," the "Absolute," "Self-Existent One."

Another instance is in the matter of God's faithfulness. That God is faithful does not mean that he is immutable in the metaphysical sense:

> Whereas the Greek philosophers understood the eternal and immutable being of God in terms of immobility and impassibility, the thought of the O.T. interpreted it in terms of His everlasting faithfulness and steadfastness in His dealings with His people, in His activities of providence and salvation.[16]

These are other instances of philosophical categories taking precedence over the biblical.

It is also a common notion that anthropomorphisms in the Bible are dated and naive ways of speaking about God, expressions to eventually be superceded by more exact terms. Such is not the case.

Scholars agree that these expressions are not inferior ways of speaking about God; they are not simply "early stages of development," nor should they even be considered as being on some kind of lower level of primitive or "naive" talk.

> How out of place it is here to speak of 'naivety'....Christian talk of God, of the 'personal God,' is often so regarded. For that reason it is classified under the head of pre-philosophic talk of the gods which perforce vanishes into thin air with enlightenment and reflection. It does in actual fact have a certain 'naivety' about it. Yet it is not the naivety of primitive ideas, which must disappear with enlightenment, but it is the naivety of every personal relation, which reflection does not resolve but only makes us conscious of its peculiar nature.[17]

If, in our relationships with our friends, we started calling them "the existing ones," I do not think we would see that as a particular improvement! Just so with God.

There is considerable agreement about the fact that a *loss* of these anthropomorphic expressions is a sign of religious decadence. G. van der Leeuw says: "The one-sided opposition to anthropomorphisms is always a sign of rationalism and religious decadence."[18]

> The anthropomorphisms are evidence of the inadequacy of human speech about God, but they also bear witness to the living relation that compels the faithful to speak of him. Wherever there is knowledge of God, communion with God, all reserves imposed by reason are abandoned, consciously or unconsciously, and human feelings and a human shape are attributed to God without any hesitation.[19]

Vreizen expresses one of the main points of this present book when he says:

> These concrete ways of representing God do not spring from a lack of spiritual insight but from a *different psychological approach to things* (Ital. mine), resulting in an entirely different outlook upon life and completely different world-picture.[20]

It is a question of *different kinds* of knowledge about God, flowing from different psyches and views of reality. The God of the Hebrews is intimately bound up with all the events of their lives, and thus their knowledge of him flows from this relation:

> Men come to know him by obeying Him in merciful and righteous acts. In the Bible, knowledge of God is not an intellectual or philosophical comprehension, like the *theoria* of the Greeks, but fellowship with Him through obedient acceptance of His sovereignty and kingship.[21]

The fact that God chose to reveal himself to us by giving personal names is also exremely significant. Names flow from relationships. We all received names shortly after our birth. But this is not naming in its true sense. As we go on in life, people often give us (albeit peculiar!) "nick-names" which flow from their experience of us. We often name people as we experience them.

God, in his providence, chose rather to have a name than to remain nameless. He could have chosen the Greeks as his special people, and made their way of conceiving him the foundation of revelation and the model for all others. But he did not. He chose the Hebrews. He chose a people who because of their whole psychological make-up would be led to give him a name. Our God deems it best that he should have a name.

Are we closer to the truth about God when we say that we know him through experience and the revelation of the name? I believe we are. But the experience we are talking about is a *cumulative experience* of God down through the ages. It is not simply the experience of God's people as expressed in the Old or New Testaments, although these are normative. It is, as we quoted Eichrodt earlier, "an ever fresh and unique delineation of the knowledge of God." The experience of one person or of only one age cannot express God's name. As man's life with God continues—as he continues to "be with us" (Ex. 3:14)—God's name becomes clearer.

God's bestowing a name on himself is very significant for several reasons:

> By his own act of bestowing a name on Himself, God chooses to be described as the definable, the distinctive, the individual. In this way the faith of Israel sets its face against both an abstract concept of deity and a nameless 'ground of being.' Both the intellectualist and the mystical misunderstanding of God are rejected.[22]
>
> The name becomes nothing less than an alternative term for Yahweh himself. The idea that in the Name is comprehended the spiritual and personal activity of Yahweh, that aspect of his being which he turns towards the world....[23]

I think these two observations are of extreme importance for theology. By "intellectualist" it is clear that Eichrodt means "philosophical" and "metaphysical" thinking. God does not reveal himself in such categories in the Bible. "Mystical" is connected with "nameless ground of being." I apply it also to any form of "mysticism" which attempts to stop thinking altogether as an approach to God.

Both of these approaches are attempts to *get behind the name*, to another essence which the name is hiding. The rational intellect scoots around the name and tries to come up with characteristics of God deduced by logic. The mystic edges his way around the name and loses himself in contemplation. Each of these ways can help to complement the knowledge of the Name, but they are not substitutes for it. Individuals may be inspired by God to emphasize one of these ways on their journey toward him, but it is always the Name which remains as the surest and most common means. It is the medium God himself chose to educate his people as regards his nature. The name reveals the essence; the icon shares in the reality.

The deepest revelation is in the name. To allow the name to take hold of one is to be more in touch conceptually with God than by relating to conclusions of syllogisms or resting in the non-thinking states. (I say "conceptually" so as not to make love a matter of having the right thoughts or non-thoughts about God.) What is being argued for is that personal names—Yahweh, Father—are more perfect expressions of who God is than abstractions.

> Only in reference to him, who has spoken to Israel and revealed himself as Yahweh, as 'he who will be,' is the word 'God' irreplaceable; for, thanks to its having been reserved for him in the history of linguistic usage, it points to himself and is a better and shorter means of calling to mind his uniqueness and superiority, his majesty and his grace, than other titles that do not have the distinction of having been reserved in the same way in the history of language. 'God' is certainly a 'symbol for God'....For biblical thought, however, that

means: 'God' is a symbol for Yahweh, i.e., if anyone wishes to say what the worldwide title 'God' as used by biblical Christian faith is *properly* supposed to mean, then the one thing he must *not* do is to speak of 'being itself' or of 'what unconditionally concerns us,' as if these were more proper designations of the One in question, but he must speak of Yahweh. Yahweh is the meaning of the symbolic word 'God' as the bible understands it.[24]

What, then, is the final answer to the question of anthropomorphisms? What do they really mean? Are they poetic images for the "real" nature of God which is arrived at by means of philosophical inquiry? Do they represent aspects of God's nature to which philosophical concepts must conform? The question, it seems to me, is only resolvable if we admit of diverse ways of knowing, and admit that each way has a proper validity and function. The language about God in the bible is not inferior to philosophical language and to be subsumed under it, nor is it naive and primitive. It is *different.* If anything, it is to be given priority, guiding all other notions of God.

The language about God in the Bible is meant to safeguard the characteristics which are of God's deep essence—his personhood, his moral superiority to man. The biblical writers' interest is with piety and personal relations, not with philosophy and "exigencies of reason."

> The only tendencies to limit the Deity which [the prophets] are determined to keep at bay are those which might have a detrimental effect on man's confidence in and reverence for God alone. The man, however, who has acknowledged him as the Living and True may conceive of him in human terms in other respects without coming to harm.[25]

In subsequent centuries the intention would shift: not personal piety but intellectual exactness would be stressed. God would become logically correct but personally remote. We know that *in some sense* God must be stable and permanent—unchanging, if you will. But if this aspect of his nature is pushed to its "logical" conclusion, we wind up with a quite impersonal and even in some respects "immoral" kind of God:

> All the emotions of which men are conscious, and all human conduct corresponding to these emotions, are thrown back upon God. Now, it may be true, that from another point of view, God must be held free of all passions, and not subject to such change as is implied in one emotion succeeding to another. Still, this latter conception, if carried to its just conclusions, would reduce God to a being not only absolutely unmoral, but even impersonal. The religious mind could express its relations to God in no other way but by attributing to Him a nature similar to its own.26

The illusory quest is to think that we can speak of God in anything *but* anthropomorphic language:

> All our talk is anthropomorphic, if this word is to be taken to mean that all language is derived from the things in which man has part. That is why a way of speaking of God which...strips off the immediately anthropomorphic expressions and restricts itself to the most abstract concepts possible, is also not by any means non-anthropomorphic. *Summum ens* too, and the *Summum bonum*, and *prima causa*, and 'being itself' (Tillich), and 'spirit,' and 'the Absolute,' 'the comprehensive,' are concepts developed by *us*, constructed in the light of our own being, even if by the *via negative* or *via eminentiae*. Abstraction is no transcending of anthropomorphisms.27

Theology does itself a great disservice if it ever so slightly tends to see biblical talk about God as simply latent philosophical talk. The former is not an improper kind of God-talk; it is a different kind. It is not naive. It is the kind of language we always use when speaking of personal relationships. It is therefore more appropriate and more accurate to use this kind of language, rather than language which concerns "Being itself."

'Being-itself' is surely still less suitable in order to indicate unmistakably what the word 'God' stands for, since as a term in the language of philosophy it leads into the old error of supposing that abstract terms are less anthropomorphic and better suited to express what is properly meant by 'God' than concrete ones. It can certainly, with the necessary commentary, likewise be employed for Yahweh, but has no advantage over other designations. We can allude by way of comparison to the employment of the Logos concept in the prologue of John's Gospel. Whether it was derived more from the OT or more from the Hellenistic world, at all events it would be a misinterpretation to suppose that to the evangelist it was a more proper designation and 'Jesus Christ' was only a symbol for Logos. On the contrary, Logos is a symbol for Jesus Christ. . . .[28]

Every other word for God is a symbol for Yahweh, and for Christians a symbol for the Father of Jesus. All other characteristics of God's nature are faint symbols for those attitudes revealed in his life with his people. Conclusions from reason or philosophy which do not help to safeguard this essence as known through his Name are misguided.

5. Father

> The Apostles...did preach the Son of God, of whom men were ignorant, and His advent, to those who had been already instructed as to God; but they did not bring in another god. For if Peter had known any such thing, he would have freely preached to the Gentiles that the God of the Jews was indeed one, but the God of the Christians another....
>
> Irenaeus of Lyons, Against Heresies, III, xii. 7

> If we regard the prophetic auditions and the communion of Jesus with his disciples as the decisive models of God's dealings with men in his special approach, then particular and concrete ways of speaking have the preference over general and abstract ones, and personal ways of speaking have the preference over impersonal, neuter ones.
>
> Helmut Gollwitzer, The Existence of God As Confessed by Faith

> So old and widely used a term as 'God,' it is frequently said, should not be given a radically new meaning. Perhaps this is just; but it should be remembered that there are several ancient meanings for 'God' rather than one. Admitting that the God of some present-day philosophers is not the God of the Scholastics or of Calvin, it does not automatically follow that the new view is in hopeless disagreement with that of Jesus and the prophets. Perhaps the new view of God is really, in some respects at least, a return to the Gospel conception.
>
> Charles Hartshorne, Reality As Social Process

Our knowledge of God comes to us from the prophets and from Christ, not from the philosophers and Epicurus.

Tertullian

In order to put some of Jesus' teaching about God in the proper context, we will cover a rather broad spectrum of time: from the Exile (586 B.C.) to the end of the New Testament writings. Admittedly, this is a vast expanse of history. However, we need only survey the general trend in Judaism and in the NT to show that Jesus and the NT writers were very much in the OT tradition. In the next chapter we shall begin to witness the profound influence of Greek philosophical thought. But during the period now under consideration, we are dealing with the God of Abraham, Isaac and Jacob.

A good place to begin is with some aspects of the Priestly School's approach to the question of God. This School, which was writing immediately after the Exile, was the final editorial board of the Pentateuch. We have seen that the prophets themselves did not avoid anthropomorphisms as long as the proper reverence for and confidence in God were not in any way jeopardized or undermined. We shall see that the Priestly School was a bit more nervous about such language; yet, they did not abandon it altogether.

This School arises at a time when thinking men everywhere are seeking to purify their often too human conceptions of God. This movement was taking place among the Greeks on a large scale. The Priestly School sought to combat some of the humanizing of God prevalent in popular notions. In the Priests' thinking

> the description of God derives from an essentially *tabu*-concept, and concentrates on the unapproachable majesty of the Deity.
> In the current of priestly thought...as this may be discerned primarily in the P stratum of the Pentateuch...the

transcendence of the Godhead is developed with a clarity which either results in a complete silencing of naive anthropomorphic conceptions of God or at least supplies a powerful corrective.[1]

This trend resulted in an increased emphasis on mediators (angels) between God and man, and the exaggerated emphasis on miracles when this more remote God should break into history. These emphases do not directly concern us. What does concern us though is that

> this Priestly language about God promoted the development of conceptual theological thought and laid the foundations for a monotheism defined in abstract terms. Such a development involves the danger of losing that sense of the nearness of God which is part of the endowment of faith....[2]

It is Eichrodt's opinion that this danger, at least within rabbinic Judaism, was overcome. God still remained the God of the covenant, a very personal and living God. Connections might be made between this tendency toward transcendence and the legalism which resulted, but, again, such is not our main intent. These tendencies were precisely that—only tendencies. A brief survey of the era of Tobit and Ecclesiasticus—the intertestamental period—will not be out of place here.

Between the Exile and the Christian era there is a large body of extant literature. Some of these writings such as Malachi, Joel, Zachary, Ecclesiastes and others, found their way into the Hebrew Canon. Others such as Maccabees, Tobit, and Ecclesiasticus were in the Greek translation of the Old Testament (the Septuagint) but were not put into the Hebrew Canon. Still others such as the Book of Jubilees, the Apocalypse of Moses, and the Testament of the Twelve Patriarchs were labeled "pseudoephigrapha" and were not accepted as canonical writings at all. Each piece of writing, however, presents a view of the theological panorama of the times. A few samplings from these writings will show that a dynamically related God was still very much a part of this period's religious thinking.

Zechariah (520 B.C.) experiences Yahweh's jealousy: "Yahweh Sabaoth says this: 'I am burning with jealousy for Zion, with great anger for her sake' " (8:2). In this period Yahweh can still be seen to *change his mind* without such a conception scandalizing the people: "But now, with the remnant of this people, I am not as I was in the past" (12).

Malachi (450 B.C.) portrays the extremes of Yahweh's feelings: "I have shown my love for you, says Yahweh. But you ask, 'How have you shown your love?' Was not Esau Jacob's brother?—it is Yahweh who speaks; yet I showed my love for Jacob and my hatred for Esau. . . .(1:2). They shall be known as Unholy Land and Nation-with-which-Yahweh-is-angry-for-ever" (4).

Joel (400 B.C.): "Turn to Yahweh your God again, for he is all tenderness and compassion, slow to anger, rich in graciousness, and ready to relent. Who knows if he will not turn again, will not relent. . ." (2:12-14)?

Jonah (4th century B.C.) relates how the Ninivites believed in God and repented and how God, seeing their change of heart and their acts of penance, *changed his resolve* to destroy their city: "Who knows if God will not change his mind and relent. . .and God relented" (3:9-10). Jonah is peeved at God's kindness: "I knew that you were a God of tenderness and compassion. . .Yahweh, please take away my life. . . ." (4:2-3). Then there is that touching allegory of the castor-oil plant which Jonah grieves over. Yahweh says: "You are only upset about a castor-oil plant. . .and am I not to feel sorry for Nineveh" (4:10)?

Ecclesiastes (3rd century B.C.): "Do not allow your own words to bring guilt on you. . . .Why should a word of yours give God occasion to be angry. . . ." (5:5)?

Norman Johnson wrote a book[3] which deals with the

prayers in some of the writings of this period. He reminds us that there is no better index of man's understanding of God than in his prayers: "Learn what kind of response this man expects...and you are in a position to infer whether the individual conceives of God as being manlike or utterly different, close at hand or distant, intimate or austere and despotic."[4] For example, concerning some of the prayers found in the Books of Maccabees Johnson writes:

> The author of II Mac. praises God for the violent and bloody death of King Antiochus (1:17). This writer represents Judas and his men as calling on God to manifest his hatred, to fight on the side of the rebels (10:15), and to be 'the enemy of their enemies' (26). Thus a passionate nature is ascribed to God.[5]

Some of the other prayers of this period are especially instructive as regards the pathos of God.

In the apocryphal 4th (2nd) Book of Esdras (end of 1st century B.C.) we find these prayers:

> I know, Lord [Uriel, an angel] that the Most High is now called merciful, because he has mercy on those who have not yet come into the world; and gracious, because he is gracious to those who turn in repentance to his law; and patient, because he shows patience toward those who have sinned, since they are his works; and bountiful because he would rather give than take away; and abundant in compassion, because he makes his compassions abound more and more to those now living and to those yet to come and to those who are gone (7:62/132).
>
> Be not angry with those who are deemed worse than beasts; but love those who have always put their trust in thy glory. For we and our fathers have passed our lives in ways that bring death; but thou, because of us sinners, are merciful. For if thou hast desired to have pity on us, who have no works of righteousness, then thou wilt be called merciful. But what is man that thou art angry with him; or what is a corruptible race, that thou art so bitter against it (8:30-34)?[6]

The God of Ecclesiasticus (2nd century B.C.) is "compassionate and merciful" (2:11). Men can please him (2:16). "His compassion is great...for with him are both mercy and wrath, and his rage bears heavy on sinners" (5:6-7). Pride is hateful to him (10:6). He "the Most High detests sinners" (12:6), but "the compassion of the Lord extends to everything that lives" (18:13).

Finally, in one of the last books in the Greek OT, the Book of Wisdom (1st century B.C.), the God of feeling and the God who can be pleased by men is not absent. "Death was not God's doing. He takes no pleasure in the extinction of the living. To be—for this he created all" (1:13). It is implied here that God *does* take great delight in all living things—that he can be *pleased* by them: "He sought to please God...his soul being pleasing to the Lord" (4:1-14).

While it is true to say that in this period there is a general withdrawal from anthropomorphic expressions, these writers still clothe God with deep feeling. To quote Johnson again: "Certain prayers imply a belief that God feels something of his own dignity, something of pride and jealousy, and a love of praise—all distinctly anthropopathic."[7]

If I may be allowed a slight digression. This notion of God being pleased and delighted by praise and ritual offers fruitful ground for artists' meditations. Because the prophets saw goodness in terms of moral rectitude, and because we read the prophets so much, we also tend to equate goodness with ethical conduct. We forget that *beauty* is also a part of goodness (e.g., liturgies should be beautiful as well as "valid").

In Leviticus, the book of the Priestly School par excellence, we often hear the refrain "a pleasing odor to the Lord" (cf. 1:9, 13, 17; 2:2, 9; 3:5). True, such phrases are in the context of sin offerings, and the notion of appeasement is present. Nevertheless, the tone of the book suggests some kind of aesthetic delight which the Lord takes in the worship and the ceremonial of his people. God, in the Scriptures, delights in the beautiful creations which man fashions in his honor.

We wish to turn now to some of the rabbinical attitudes toward God in the period roughly from the Maccabean era to the fourth or fifth century A.D. To help set the stage for the Gospel teaching, I wish to give the reader a general feel for the approach of the rabbis to the question of anthropomorphisms.

It is not true that the rabbis began to consider this problem because of Hellenistic influences. Early Hebrew sources show that the rabbis were aware of the difficulty which only later appeared in Hellenistic writings.[9] They were fully cognizant of the implications and ramifications of anthropomorphic expressions about God; they were aware no doubt also of how "uncultured" this would make them appear to the philosophers.

As might be expected, there were various schools of thought. However, even at this late period we are considering (NT times), it is Marmorstein's opinion that the school which fought to *retain* anthropomorphisms was the *dominant* school and in the *majority*:

> There were two schools, one opposing, the other defending, the literality of the Biblical text on which their theological outlook depended and their conception of God was based. On the whole, one can say so at the outset, the *anthropomorphic trend of mind*, so warmly defended and propagated by R. Akiba and his followers, *gained the upper hand first, and the great number of teachers adopted his view* (Ital. mine); whilst only a small minority cherished and dared to propagate allegorical doctrines.[10]

Generally speaking, the rabbis had no strong philosophic bias. They avoided allegory. They often qualified their anthropomorphisms with phrases like "so to speak" and "in human terms." It was a question of having to speak of God in human terms: "The Torah has to make the Eternal smaller to speak of Him."[11] Or they would say, "One makes the ear hear what it can grasp, and the eye see what it can behold."[12]

Marmorstein says that it was a common teaching of the rabbis of this period that there is an intimate connection between God and Israel, so much so that God *weeps and mourns* with his people. God is also *in bondage*, and he is liberated when Israel is liberated. "The rabbis do not mind speaking of God as being in trouble or pain, thinking of Him as sharing His people's distress."[13]

> R. Akiba, the great religious teacher and the immortal national martyr of the Jewish people, is credited with the teaching that the Exodus of the Hebrew slaves from Egypt meant much more than the freeing of serfs from bondage. It signified the release of God Himself, if one may say such a thing of God. The teaching goes back to Ps. XCI. 15. God was in servitude during the whole time that His children were subjugated by the taskmasters of Pharaoh.[14]

For readers who are interested in following up this theme in the rabbis, they are referred to the section in Moltmann's recent book, *The Crucified God*. Quoting Kuhn, Moltmann writes: "The rabbis at the turn of the ages spoke of a number of stages in the self-humiliation of God: in the creation, in the call of Abraham, Isaac, and Jacob and the history of Israel, in the exodus and in the exile."[15] Then Moltmann says:

> His lamentation and sorrow over Israel in the exile show that God's whole existence with Israel is in suffering. So, conversely, the liberation of Israel also means the liberation of that 'indwelling of God' from its suffering. God has redeemed himself from Egypt together with his people: 'The redemption is for me and for you.' The suffering of God is the means by which Israel is redeemed. God himself is 'the ransom' for Israel.[16]

These notions of God suffering with Israel come from the rabbis of the time. The ramifications and application of these ideas to the suffering and death of Christ as God's definitive self-humiliation are obvious. However, this is not my concern here. My point is that the debate on anthropomorphisms was handled differently in the rabbinic schools than it was in the schools more influenced by Hellenistic thought:

> In the Greek world the idea of a personal God was regarded as a final relic of the anthropomorphic thinking which had to be overcome. In the Jewish world the distinction between anthropomorphic conceptions and faith in the personal God was not only maintained but grasped with increasing clarity. God is not as a man. But He is a God who wills and speaks and hears. The Rabbis conceived the personality of God more radically than any before them.[17]

The first fact upon which all scholars are agreed is that Jesus' conception of God and his approach to him were very much in accord with the rabbinic Judaism of his day. There are advances, but "to a considerable extent Jesus shared the views of his fellow Jews about God, who had revealed himself to Moses and to the prophets."[18] "The identity of the God of the New Testament with Yahweh, the God of the Old Testament, is everywhere assumed by New Testament writers, though they never explicitly assign to Him the name Yahweh."[19] "While his [Jesus'] doctrine about God far excels that of the prophets, it is organically continuous with the best prophetic teaching. The God of the New Testament is the God of the Old Testament reinterpreted and more fully revealed in the light of the Person and Work of Jesus Christ."[20] "So far as we can judge from the Synoptic Gospels and from his attitude reflected there, he [Jesus] did not regard it as his mission to promulgate a new God or to teach new ideas about God, but rather to summon his fellows to live as God—his God and theirs—would have them live."[21]

The early Church fought a bitter battle with Marcion over this very question—the identity of the God of both Testaments. Marcion thought he saw such a profound difference between the Old and New Testament conceptions of God that the only way he could solve his dilemma was to posit two gods, the vindictive God of the Old, and the loving God of the New. The ancient Church vigorously affirmed the identity of the two.

As mentioned earlier, we are all Marcionites at heart. We would like the God of Jesus to be pure love—which he is—but *our idea of love*! Hard as it is for us to admit or see it, there is much of the God of the Old Testament in Jesus' teaching and preaching. It is true to say, I think, that the God spoken of by Jesus in the New Testament is much closer to the God of the Old Testament than many people would care to admit! "The vast majority of believing Christians of all traditions look at God and at Jesus Christ through the spectacles of Nicea...we do not think of God as the God of the Jews...."[22]

This is a fruitful observation. We believe, of course, in our understanding of revelation and the Spirit's action, that Jesus continues to teach his people about his Father. Many of our notions about God come from this ongoing revelation. But it may also be true that other notions accumulated through the centuries have distored some aspects of our notions of God. Until recently, we did not often think of our God as "Yahweh." In many respects, our God was not very "Jewish."

Scholars also agree (this is obvious but needs to be emphasized here) that Jesus' notion of God is not philosophical but quite concrete and anthropomorphic.

We believe that Jesus spoke the truth about God and man. He spoke it, however, in a particular historical situation. Jesus spoke of God according to the rabbinic tradition of his times. His picture of God is very anthropormorphic, very much related and concerned with man, not in any way impassible or remote. The Father of Jesus is as intensely personal as ever, even more so.

> Even in the NT, though a certain contact with the atmosphere of Hellenistic culture has led to the absence of the same vivid anthropomorphisms, we are still far from a philosophic doctrine of God's immutability, not to say His impassibility . . .the fundamental NT doctrine of God's Fatherhood suggests the very reverse of His impassibility.[23]

It is in this area of personality where Jesus' teachings about God are deepened and receive their distinctive characteristics. Many authors see the uniqueness of Jesus' revelation about God not so much in new ideas about him as in intensifying certain aspects already in Judaism. The God of Jesus is *even more personal than the God of the OT*, and we saw that this personhood of Yahweh was the primary revelational fact about God in the OT.

Furthermore, the intensification of the personality of God for Jesus lies in his unique use of the name of Father. When I say "unique use" I do not mean to imply that God was never called "Father" in the OT or among the rabbis of the times. There are a variety of opinions as to just how Jesus used the name "Father" differently than others.

McGiffert tends to see great similarity between Jesus and his contemporaries in this regard. He says that it was common in Jesus' time to call God, Father. This title suggested affection, but also sovereignty and power.

> It naturally suggested God's care for his people and their answering love and obedience, but often it seems to have been used as any other word might have been used, with no thought of a special significance attaching to it. As one of the common names for God, it might easily be so used.[24]

Montefiore believes that there was much more uniqueness about Jesus' use of the name Father: "We certainly do not get in the Hebrew Bible any teacher speaking of God and to God as 'Father,' 'my Father,' 'your Father' and 'our Father,' like the Jesus of Matthew."[25] Using this statement of Montefiore's, Williams made this question the basis of a brief but in-depth study of the question. He asked:

> Now what evidence is there in the Judaism of the first century or thereabouts of the individualistic apprehension of the Fatherhood of God? I mean, what evidence is there of the use of 'my God,' not 'our God'; and further of 'my God' not merely because the speaker knows himself to be a member of the nation of Israel, but as having direct and personal relationship with God as his Father? Frankly, there is extraordinary little of such evidence. The phrase, in our meaning of it as thus defined, occurs nowhere in the Old Testament.[26]

This author then goes on to cite passages in both the OT and in rabbinic literature of the times where the word Father is used of God. He concludes: "Still the fact remains, that for one cause or another during the early centuries neither on Jewish nor on Christian lips is the phrase 'my Father' other than a rare and isolated expression."[27]

If the question is then asked, "What did Jesus add to the understanding of God?" it seems correct to say that he gave the name Father a deeper and more profound significance than it ever had before—and this both in relation to himself and to others.

Jesus used the name Father in a variety of contexts. While it is not his most frequent name for God, it certainly was his *favorite* one. It is the name he preferred when he taught his disciples to pray; it is the name he used whenever he spoke intimately to God, as for instance in his hour of trial in the garden. On the lips of Jesus this name indicates the

> consciousness of a relationship deeper and more intimate, a relationship extending beyond the possibility of the merely human, reaching up to such a connexion with the divine as had, in fact, existed before He came into the world. This...is

clearly the opinion of the writer of the Fourth Gospel. I have no doubt myself that it is also the opinion of each of the three writers of the synoptic Gospels, including St. Mark.28

What Jesus does then is raise the Fatherhood of God to an intensity that it did not have before. "The divine fatherhood was realized by Jesus with the utmost clearness and intimacy. He would have wished that all his disciples should have realized that fatherhood as closely and fully as he...."29

In other words, Jesus revealed the *true paternity* of the Father. "The Father's love as revealed by Jesus is more personal and more passionate than in the Old Testament."30

> Jesus brought to the world the certitude that God was truly Father for men, and that men would really be able to become his sons. Consequently, just as in the order of nature, the words father and son signify a stronger and more intimate love, with mutual rights and obligations, so in the kingdom of God which Jesus came to establish on earth, there ought to exist between God and humanity paternal and filial relations of love, and the members of the kingdom have the power to become the children of God.31

We can say that Jesus raised the relational, the caring, the pathos of God for man to its greatest intensity. Jesus is aware of the most intimate relationship with his Father, and he desires and preaches that this is possible for all men.

The Father of Jesus cares deeply for the unjust as well as for the just. He cares for everything from wicked men to the lilies of the field and the birds of the air. This Father waits for the sinner's return as any heart-sick parent would do. When the prodigal finally returns, this Father runs to meet him, hugs and kisses him.

In many of his parables Jesus continues the teaching of the OT that "God is not like a man," that is, that God *in his moral attitudes* far transcends man's ways of acting. The parables of the Workers in the Vineyard and of the Prodigal Son were so enigmatic to Jesus' audience because God's ways of acting do not conform to ordinary human standards. We can almost hear Jesus commenting after these stories, in confirmation of the words of the prophet, "Do you think God is like *you*?"

As little as we like to advert to it, there is much of the God of justice and punishment in Jesus' teaching about the Father. In the synoptic gospels Jesus does not once mention explicitly the love of God. Of course, that God loves us is inseparable from the stories Jesus tells, and from his call to be sons of God (Mt 5:45). Still, a great deal of Jesus' teaching and preaching concerns judgment and God's severity with sinners (Mt 12:31ff.; 15:3ff.; Mk 8:38; 11:15; Lk 10:15; 11:29).[32] God's wrath is as plain in the parables of Jesus as it is in Pauline theology.

It also seems true to say that the transcendentalizing tendency of the Priestly school is not encouraged by Jesus. The most common name for God in the rabbinic literature of the times is "the Holy One," a name which reflects this tendency.[33] Jesus does not once use this title for God. Nor do the angels as intermediaries between man and a rather remote God play any part in Jesus' teachings.

McGiffert sums up for us this present section: "God was always strictly personal for Jesus—Ruler, Judge, Master, Lord, Father. He thought of him in anthropomorphic, not in metaphysical or mystical fashion."[34] And Grant says: "To a considerable extent Jesus shared the views of his fellow Jews about God who had revealed himself to Moses and to the prophets. What characterizes him is all-inclusive love."[35] Again, it is the strong and powerful love of *God* Jesus preaches, not our often over-sentimental notion.

What about the other New Testament writers? How do they speak about God? Generally, "they content themselves, in accordance with the teaching of Jesus, to state that the name of 'Father' is God's special name.... they neglect almost entirely to reveal other traits which characterize the nature of God and his perfections."[36] When the Apostles in Acts speak to their fellow Jews, they speak of the God of Abraham, Isaac, and Jacob (3:13; 22:14). He is the God of the people of Israel (13:17), the God who appeared to Abraham (7:2); he is Father (2:33).

Paul's God, too, is generally the God of Jesus, though, in accordance with Jesus' promise, the Spirit continues to reveal the fullness of what Jesus taught. Paul, under the Spirit's guidance, develops the implications of the Fatherhood of God by speaking of the adoption as sons which flows from our union with Jesus. Paul speaks more of the love of God than Jesus did. Also, Paul still knows the anger of God (Rm 1:18; 2:5-6); Co 3:5-6: "...that is why you must kill everything in you that belongs only to earthly life...all this sort of behavior makes God angry." Hebrews speaks of our pleasing God. God is pleased by our faith (11:6), and by our sacrifices of mutual help (13:16). In the earliest document in the New Testament, First Thessalonians, God can be pleased (2:4).

As might be expected, the Letter of James still breathes the vibrant faith of the Old Testament and the Judaic mind. Yahweh is very much in relationship with his people, as jealous and compassionate as ever: "You are as unfaithful as adulterous wives; don't you realize that making the world your friend is making God your enemy? Surely you don't think Scripture is wrong when it says, 'The Spirit which he sent to live in us wants us for himself alone' " (4:4). This passage cannot be traced with certainty, but it is evident how much it is in keeping with the whole prophetic tradition. Mozley comments on these and similar passages: "We cannot evade the conclusion that to this extent change is conceived of as actual in God, that wrath can give place to the free exercise of love."[37] He is speaking about the New Testament. Also in James the "cries of the reapers have reached the ears of the Lord"

(5:4). God, therefore, is still very compassionate, being moved by the cries of the poor and the defenseless.

The question may arise in one's mind: since, by the time of the New Testament, we are already three-hundred years into the Hellenization process of the ancient world, are there any philosophical doctrines or modes of thought about God in these early Christian writings that found their way into the Canon?

It is Grant's opinion that while there are no philosophical doctrines about God in the NT, there are what he calls "philosophical bridges," that is, the use of philosophical terms which later Christian writers would seize upon and develop. He mentions 1 Co 8, Rm 1:19-21, 1 Tm 1:17, and Ga 4:8-10 as instances of such bridges. It is not germaine to our present topic to enter into his justification of these views.

What is relevant is his main conclusion, namely, that while there are a few philosophical terms, there is no attempt to arrive at God's existence or attributes *through purely philosophical means.* For the NT writers, "there is no real knowledge of God apart from revelation; there is no real knowledge of God apart from grace; there is no real knowledge of God apart from faith."[38]

Grant has some further remarks on the text from 1 Jn 4:8 that "God is love"; we have called attention to this before. He says that "later philosophical theologians were going to have great difficulty with this text. From the writings of the early Christians after the NT we can discover relatively few references to God's love."[39] The main reason for this is that the age was preoccupied with the question of God's transcendence and his relation to the cosmos.[40] The questions about God with which Christian writers had to deal centered mainly in this area. "We shall see how conscious of God's transcendence and of man's limitations the early Christians were, and how difficult they found it to make sense of the basic affirmation that God is love."[41]

This is indeed a curious feature of early Christian

writing and thinking on the nature of God. Nowadays most people like to think of John's profound sentence—"God is love"—as the epitome of the NT revelation about God. It is a truth that appeals to our deepest aspirations and hopes: that God is Pure Love. Yet, there is scarcely any attempt to develop this insight: "(the doctrine of God in the 2nd century) appears to have been made in its earliest form virtually without the assistance of that document which was deliberately preparing the way for such a transposition, the Gospel of St. John; and we can see how much it suffered from the lack of this Gospel."[42]

A recent study has just appeared. In Burton Cooper's *The Idea of God,* which we quoted earlier, he argues for the passibility of God on the grounds of an ontology of love. It is Cooper's opinion that the Platonic ontology of the early Christian centuries did not mix well with the revelation of God as love:

> If love means the vulnerability of one being to the suffering of another, if it entails the risk of openness, the possibility of loss, and the hope of value, then Patristic thought never fully developed an ontology of love. What I would like to argue now is that when orthodoxy turned to the task of working out an aspect of the idea of God peculiar to Biblical faith, namely the Trinitarian dogma, the ontology implied by that dogma turns out to be quite at variance with the Hellenic ontology underlying the doctrine of the divine perfections.[43]

The reader is referred to this book for Cooper's approach to the problem. It is very fascinating. Working out the implications of "God is love" will be one of the approaches in exploring the pathos of God in the future of theology.

We have come to the end of our survey of the NT period and the preceding few centuries. The groundwork has now been prepared to look at the other currents of thought at work. Hanson sums up well for us our present juncture:

> The Bible does not supply us with a complete and consistent and philosophically viable Christian doctrine of God. It presents the reader with the doctrine of God of late ancient Judaism on the one hand, and on the other with a number of statements about somebody called Jesus Christ. But it makes only the most rudimentary program towards integrating these two things, towards producing a doctrine of God which is specifically and recognizably Christian.[44]

What is surprising for anyone studying the notion of God in the scriptures is, as Hanson says, how undefined, how open-ended is the reality of God. So many of the notions we have about God come from other regions of human culture and thought.

A good example is the notion which is of special interest to us in this book, the "impassibility" of God. Grant says that "the word *apathes* 'impassible' does not occur in the New Testament."[45] God is "invisible, powerful, eternal, and imperishable,"[46] but not impassible! Where did the notion come from? Ultimately it comes from the Greeks; more proximately, for Christians, it comes (according to many authors) from *Hellenistic Judaism.*

6. The Unchangeable

> For what greater impiety could there be than to suppose that the Unchangeable changes?
>
> Philo of Alexandria, *The Unchangeableness of God*

> Hellenistic thought inevitably influenced Judaism...its most typical and successful expression is to be found in the writings of Philo of Alexandria.
>
> Richard A. Norris, *God and the World In Early Christian Theology*

> In the extravagance of his recoil from materialism Philo transformed the good Father and Lord of the Bible into the Eternal Negation of dialectics.
>
> Charles Bigg, *The Christian Platonists of Alexandria*

We travel now to the city of Alexandria during the time immediately before Christ and the century contemporaneous with him. Never before had the ancient world seen such a modern city. Three miles long and a mile wide, Strabo tells us, with thoroughfares and lighted streets, shaded colonnades and main arteries linking every part of the city. There were administrative buildings, government houses, a thousand shops and bazaars. Outside the gates were a stadium, a hippodrome or race track, and an amphitheater.

About the year 2000 B.C. Alexandria was a modern metropolis with about five hundred thousand Macedonians, Greeks, Egyptians, Jews, Persians, Anatolians, Syrians, Arabs, and Negroes. The ideas of these peoples intermingled in some of the greatest centers of learning in the ancient world. In this city stood the world's greatest library. "It was not without reason," Bigg says, "that the first systematic attempt to harmonize the tradition of faith with the free conclusions of human intellect was made neither at Rome nor at Athens, but in Egypt."[1]

Alexandria was one of the *"diaspora"* situations of the Jews. They lived in the northeast portion of the city. Jewish settlements dating from the seventh century have been found in Egypt when the Jews entered in the wake of the Persian invasion. It is estimated that by the beginning of the Christian era there were a million Jews in Alexandria, and they lived, as was their custom, in many intellectual and cultural ghettoes; there was also great pressure on them to become hellenized to alleviate the threat of Jewish dominance.

It was here, in Alexandria, that the merger of Jewish and Greek thought began. However, we must always remember that the phenomenon of Hellenization had been going on for three hundred years by the time of Philo and Jesus, who were contemporaries.

Philo the Jew, born in Alexandria about 25 B.C., at the height of the city's glory, was one of the wealthiest men of his day. We know definitely of one instance where he pleaded with the Emperor Gaius on behalf of the Jewish people threatened by massacre. Only a man of outstanding means could have been chosen for such a task. His writings show that he was intimately in touch with all aspects of the teeming life of Alexandria. He was married, had slaves, and possessed a considerable amount of leisure time for writing and intellectual pursuits. He died sometime between 45 and 50 A.D.

The aspect of Hellenization with which we are concerned—the modification of the biblical notion of God—no doubt began with the use of the Greek language to explain the scriptures during the synagogue services. In these local church gatherings there was a simple service of prayers, songs, readings from the scriptures and homilies. (All Christians owe the basic format of their own liturgy of the word to the Jewish synagogue service.) In earliest times the scriptures were read in Hebrew; then a homily would be given in the vernacular (Greek). Before long there was a need for a Greek translation of the Hebrew Scriptures.

The tradition behind the translation of the Hebrew scriptures into Greek is well known. About 250 B.C. Ptolemy Philadelphus invited seventy scholars to take up the work. Each scholar (so the tradition goes!) went into a separate room, did the translation, and when all came together again, all the translations matched perfectly. However it happened, this *Interpretatio Septuaginata Seniorum*, the "Interpretation of the Seventy Elders," or, as it became commonly known, the *Septuagint* (LXX), was the official Greek translation of the Old Testament, at least in Alexandria. Thus the Pentateuch, the first five books of the bible, appeared in Greek before the close of the third century.

No doubt there were other translations. What is important for us is that the Septuagint was the bible of Philo. It is disputed whether Philo knew Hebrew or not; most likely he did. Whatever the answer to that, Philo spoke Greek. The Septuagint was his daily, reading bible, and he believed that the *translation* was just as inspired as the original work. For our purposes, that is very important to remember.

Philo was a good Jew. In what follows we do not wish to imply in any way that Philo set out to change the traditional content of his faith. It is also disputed by scholars whether he was an original genius, or more of a spokesman for a longer tradition. One gets the impression from reading his works that he might have been both. He certainly wrote a tremendous amount!

What I *will* contend, however, is that in Philo's works we come across a real change in the concept of God. We could say that there is a transition, mentioned by Murray, from speaking about God in biblical, personalist, relational categories, to philosophical, essentialist ones. Other Jews had probably done this before, but none of Philo's stature. Says Danielou: "Philo is a theologian—and unquestionably the first theologian to treat fully of the divine transcendence."[2]

The "change" in Philo's notion of God needs to be further specified. Both the Father and "the Existant," the philosophical description, are in Philo. He is a groundbreaker (or a representative of the ground-breaking), one who reflects the transitional phase midway between Yahweh and "Being."

Lest the reader, who may be unfamiliar with Philo, thinks that with him we are dealing with a marginary figure on the intellectual scene, it should be pointed out that no less an authority than Wolfson (who wrote a two-volume work on Philo), claims that he was the one who laid the philosophical, religious and psychological foundations for Western philosophy and theology which lasted for seventeen hundred years!

This sounds like quite a claim—and it surely is. But scholars are generally agreed that Philo's works were widely read in the first centuries of Christianity. Later on we shall see the direct dependence of Clement of Alexandria on Philo. Christians saw in his works a successful merger of the Greek-Biblical synthesis with which they also were struggling.

Philo was a great preacher. His works are basically commentaries on the scriptures. Some think that many of his treatises were perhaps given in a synagogue setting. Thus, he is a kind of Jewish exegete of the New Testament times. There is even a slight possibility that his writings influenced John or Paul.

There is a basic agreement among scholars that Philo was concerned with combining Greek metaphysics with the biblical revelation. Bigg remarks that "it was in the mind of the Jew that Eastern and Western ideas were first blended into fruitful union." The object of the hellenizing party was to "appropriate Greek wisdom, and to justify the appropriation; to reconcile Judaism with the culture of the Western world." We associate these ideas with Philo because he is to us their sole exponent.3

All the intricacies of this project we leave to the scholars. What I hope to present, with their help, are some of the rather clear lines and contours of the enterprise with regard to the attribute of God's "impassibility." What I further wish to emphasize is that, whatever Philo intended, the results of his thinking about the nature of God led, in some respects, further and further away from any kind of pathos in him.

There has always been an unclear answer to the question of how the synthesis between the Christian message and Hellenism could have been made so quickly. For most people this is a non-problem. But for those who trace the history of ideas, their genesis, growth, and inter-dependencies, some fundamental decisions were made seemingly very quickly on how to use the Greek wisdom in relation to Christianity. More and more scholars are coming to the conclusion that the answer lies in Hellenistic Judaism.

For hundreds of years, in places like Alexandria, and by people like Philo and his predecessors, thinkers had been grappling with the problems. To get a taste of this Hellenistic Judaism, we will review briefly some of E. R. Goodenough's ideas about Philo and his methodology. It will give the reader some indication of how a Greek-thinking Jew, dedicated to his own biblical revelation, tried to work out the truths about God, the world and man.

Philo was equally fascinated by both the Bible and the philosophical schools. He read Plato in terms of Moses and Moses in terms of Plato. The Jews, according to Philo, had a *superior form* of the truths expressed in Greek metaphysics. Conveying the thoughts of Heinemann, Goodenough remarks that Philo saw the superiority of

Judaism as one of *degree.* Through the *allegorical method* one could find in the Torah the truths of the Greeks. The Torah was a "cryptogram of Greek thought."[4]

Philo tried to remain true to his own traditions and to the Greek wisdom. But I believe the facts will show that the following is what happened: *the Greek idea became the truth of which the biblical language was a symbol.* Or, to use Gollwitzer's phrasing, Yahweh became a symbol for Being, and not Being a symbol for Yahweh. Instead of seeing both the Greek idea and the Hebrew anthropomorphisms as expressing two aspects of God, the latter became the image of the former; the Greek idea became the "real" truth.

We are dealing with a concept put into another language. The people who make the substitution may be able to keep the original idea while using different words; they have integrated the two currents. But what about the people who read this new word—for example, *Kyrios*—70, 100, 300, or a 1,000 years later? These later generations may neither know Hebrew nor have any Jewish culture or background—no existential knowledge of Yahweh. Will not the new word connote to these people very different meanings? Because it is technical, I quote a rather long passage from Wolfson which describes what the Septuagint translators did with the words for God:

> In the Greek translation of the Bible, when the translators came to translate the various Hebrew terms for God, they did not attempt to coin new Greek terms; they borrowed terms already used in Greek religion. *Elohim* becomes *theos,* even though the Greek term had already various connotations in Greek religion. *Adonai* and *Jehovah*...are translated *kurios,* Lord, even though in later Greek literature that term is used as an epithet of various gods. *Shaddai* becomes *pantocrator,* almighty, even though, again, in Greek literature, that term is used of Hermes. The expression *ha-El ha-Gadol,* the great God, is translated by *o theos o megas.* ...The expression *El Elyon,* the most high God, is translated by *o theos o uphistos,* even

though in Greek that expression is used of Zeus. All of these of course meant some sort of Hellenization, but a Hellenization in language only; not in religious belief or cult.[5]

The question is, "Can there be a hellenization in language only?" For future generations it seems not. Besides, as we shall see, the translators went beyond a mere word substitution. They changed concepts.

Danielou informs us that one of the concerns of the translators of the Septuagint was to eliminate anthropomorphisms which did not seem worthy of God. Some examples. Ex 24: 10 in the Hebrew reads, "They saw the God of Israel." In the Greek translation it becomes, "They saw the *place* where the God of Israel. . . ." In a text which Philo will use extensively, Gn 6:6, we have in the Hebrew, "And God repented." In the Greek it becomes a bland "He had it in his mind."

Another procedure along these same lines was to replace images with abstract expressions (replace the right with the left hemisphere!). There are many examples. The hand of God becomes the power of God. The shield of God becomes the help of God (Ps 7:10). God as a rock becomes a support (Ps 18:3).

Still a third procedure was to attribute to *angels* what the Hebrew text attributes to God. (We saw that the use of angels in this way is a result of the transcendentalizing process.) In Ex 4:24 the Hebrew text has, "On the journey, when Moses had halted for the night, Yahweh came to meet him and tried to kill him." The Septuagint has, "the angel of Yahweh tried to kill him." The Hebrew for Ps 8:6: "You have made him a little less than God," becomes in the Septuagint, "You have made him a little less than the angels." (Some of the newer translations have gone back to the original Hebrew.)

Thus the Septuagint reveals a universal attempt to adapt to the Greek taste. Nature is described in more scientific and less animistic terms. And the classic text from Ex 3:14 (the best Hebrew translations of which we have already seen) becomes here for the first time "I am who am." The dynamic name of Yahweh is translated in terms of Platonic ontology. This orientates the phrase in terms of an ontological essentialism.[6]

Thus Philo is heir to an increasing Hellenization, an ongoing transcendentalism concerning the notion of God. Danielou says that it was in the development of the theology of God's transcendence that the influence of Hellenistic Judaism was at its most pronounced upon the Judaeo-Christian movement.[7] "This attempt of the LXX to discard as far as possible the Old Testament anthropomorphisms is...a dubious undertaking."[8]

There were other Hellenistic Jews before Philo. They reveal a transition from scripture to Philo. That is, a transition from the biblical God to Philo's more philosophical one. In Aristeas, for example, "the Jewish God indeed is incorporeal and free of emotions as is the God of the philosophers, but still he is not without personal relation to man."[9] Philo will go one step further and claim that God "has no relations...that He wants nothing, and depends on nothing, because He is perfect and the source of all that is."[10]

Philo, as has been mentioned, is a biblical exegete. He did not write treatises on specific subjects. Thus his doctrine on God is scattered throughout his works. I will quote from only one of his works here because it is most directly related to the pathos of God. Further on I will give aspects of his doctrine on God which relate to his general tendency to emphasize the transcendence of God.

The work we will look at here is called *The Unchangeableness of God (Quod Deus Immutabilis)*.[11] It is really part of a larger treatise on certain books of Genesis. Philo uses many terms for God in this treatise—the Existent One, the Cause of all, the One and the Monad, the truly Existent, God. The words represent the transitional phase we spoke of earlier and Philo's own intellectual struggle. I believe, however, that the "Existent" finally won out over the Father. Let Philo speak for himself.

Genesis 6:7 speaks of God "regretting" that he had made man. Philo comments: "Some on hearing these words suppose that the Existant feels wrath and anger, whereas He is not susceptible to any passion at all." Earlier, in connection with the same passage, he had said: "For what greater impiety could there be than to suppose that the Unchangeable changes?" And further on: "Can you doubt that He, the Imperishable One, who has taken as His own the sovereignty of the virtues, of perfection, and beatitude, knows no change of will, but ever holds fast to what He purposed from the first without any alteration?"

According to Philo, then, how do we explain such language which implies that God changed his mind? He says that such language is purely pedagogical: "The Lawgiver [Moses] uses such expressions, just so far as they serve for a kind of elementary lesson, to admonish those who could not otherwise be brought to their senses."

A good example of Philo's bias is seen in how he treats the verse from Numbers, that "God is not a man" (23:19). Philo writes: "There stand forth...two leading statements about the Cause, one 'that God is not as a man'...; the other that He is 'as a man' (Dt 8:5). But while the former is warranted by grounds of surest truth, the latter is introduced for the instruction of the man. And thus it is for training and admonition, not because God's nature is such that these words are used."

How does Philo know that these words do not refer to God's nature "as such"? I believe it is because he knows the Greek philosophical teaching about the immutability of the "real" world of ideas, and therefore of God. It follows that "God is not as a man" is of the surest truth;

the other, that he is "like a man" is a mere pedagogical device. He says that those who are educated will understand this.

The reader will forgive the following long quotation from Philo, but I think it is very instructive for an insight into Philo's position and method:

> Among men some are soul lovers, some body lovers. The comrades of the soul, who can hold converse with the intelligible incorporeal natures, do not compare the Existant to any form of created things. They have disassociated Him from every category or quality, for it is one of the facts which go to make His blessedness and supreme felicity that His being is apprehended as simple being, without definite characteristic; and thus they do not picture it with form, but admit to their minds the conception of existence only. But to those who have made a compact and a truce with the body are unable to cast off from them the garment of flesh, and to descry existence needing nothing in its unique solitariness, and free from all admixture and composition in its absolute simplicity. And therefore they think of the Cause of all in the same terms as of themselves, and do not reflect that while a being which is formed through the union of several faculties needs several parts to minister to the need of each, God being uncreated and the Author of the creation of others needs none of the properties which belong to the creatures He has brought into being.
>
> For consider, if He uses our bodily parts or organs, He has feet to move from one place to another. But whither will He go or walk since His presence fills everything? To whom will He go, when none is His equal? And for what purpose will He walk? For it cannot be out of care of health as it is with us. Hands He must have to receive and give. Yet He receives nothing from anyone, for, besides that He has no needs, all things are His possessions, and when He gives, He employs as minister of His gifts the Reason wherewith also He made the world. These are the mythical fictions of the impious, who, professing to represent the deity as of human form, in reality represent Him as having human passions.

Here we have a perfect statement of the two epistemologies at work in Philo concerning the knowledge of God. In all fairness to Philo, it seems that many of the biblical writers would have to be classified as "body lovers" and also as "impious," since much of their knowledge of God flowed from their physical sensibilities. For Philo, only the *mind* can attain to God's nature: "But He is not apprehensible even by the mind, save in the fact that He is. For it is His existence which we apprehend, and of what lies outside that existence, nothing." On this aspect of Philo's teaching Goodenough rightly says, for Philo, "God is, and nothing can be said of deity except this. He, or It, is utterly self-contained and self-sufficient."[12]

These passages, I think, are enough to give the reader a taste of Philo's general attitude toward God.

The so-called "negative theology" approach to God, that is, saying he is uncreated, incomprehensible, unbounded, unknowable, etc., also stems from Philo. It was to become the heritage of the early Greek Church. Danielou says: "[Philo is] unquestionably the first theologian to treat fully of the divine transcendence. It was no longer enough to demonstrate, in opposition to popular paganism, that God was spiritual; it was also necessary to prove his transcendence in order to combat philosophical rationalism. In this field Philo made a considerable contribution to the creation of a vocabulary for use in negative statements about God."[13] I am not implying, of course, that this approach is not valid, or one way to speak of God. The danger is that it is substituted for the biblical way instead of complementing it.

The question of the use and abuse of *allegory* was a bone of contention in the early Church. We must look briefly at Philo's contribution to this area because it has much to do with our topic.

Bigg says: "Other parts of his [Philo's] legacy were more questionable still—his vicious Allegorism, his theory of the Absolute God."[14] Allegory is basically the interpretation of one text by means of something else. To use allegory in regard to the scriptures was a legitimate method practiced by the rabbis. What Philo introduces, according to Wolfson and others, is a *new kind of allegory*, namely, *philosophical allegory*. "In their new environment some Alexandrian Jews came into possession of a new body of knowledge derived from Greek philosophy, and out of this new body of knowledge they developed a new method of the interpretation of Scripture...."[15] Philo says that if you do not use this method, many statements about God would be objectionable. He cites the Genesis passage (6:6) and says that those who refuse to use the philosophical allegorical method are unthinking persons and full of inconsistencies.[16]

Philo uses this allegorical method without reserve. One of his general rules is that no anthropomorphic expression about God is to be taken literally. To emphasize again one of my main contentions, I believe it is at junctures such as this in the history of thought that something went awry. Anthropomorphisms are a *different way of knowing*, and express some deep truth about God. If this is not appreciated or accepted, then they must be interpreted *in terms of something else.* What is this "something else"? For Philo, it was the conclusions of Greek metaphysics. Indeed, G. F. Moore goes so far as to say that the conceptions of both the immateriality of God and of monotheism as a doctrine of the unity of God in the metaphysical sense are derived from Philo. And Philo derived these doctrines "from Plato, and reads them into the Bible with the rest of his philosophy; but he did not get them from the Bible or from Judaism at all."[17]

We do not wish to be too hard on Philo. His writings show that he knew both the related, "religiously available" God who is Father and full of compassion for his children, and the abstract, philosophical God of his philosophy. The truth seems to be that it was the latter God who dominated.

Drummond says that the solitary independence of God is stressed in the strongest possible way in Philo. Quoting the latter: "The Self-existant Being regarded simply as self-existant, does not come under the category of relation; for it is full of itself, and sufficient to itself, equally both before and after the creation of the universe; for it is unchangeable, requiring nothing else at all, so that all things belong to it, but it, strictly speaking, to nothing." (Note the use of the neuter "it" in reference to God!)

Drummond interprets Philo's doctrine of relation as a kind of one-sided relation. Dependence is all on one side, and that not the divine side. Again and again in Philo we come across the notion of God's "exhaustive completeness." Philo says: "The full God is in need of nothing, and cannot be benefited by human service"; "He is all the most precious things to himself, kindred, relation, friend, virtue, blessedness, happiness, knowledge, understanding, beginning, end, whole, all, judge, opinion, counsel, law, action, sovereignty"; God "the most self-sufficing, is in need of nothing else."[18]

Philo does speak of the "wrath of God" in a serious passage. Drummond comments:

> But in doing so [i.e., speaking of God's wrath] there can be no doubt that he consciously used language which did not correspond with his philosophical thought, and that he meant only to express that passionless opposition to sin which we may reasonably ascribe to the Divine; for, as we have seen, he believed that the use of this kind of inadequate or erroneous language was necessary, and in regard to this very passion of anger, he says elsewhere that it is properly predicated of men, but only figuratively of the Self-Existent.[19]

Several authors point out this struggle in Philo's thinking between the God of Israel and the God of the philosophers. "Far as Philo went in accepting the abstract Pure Being of the Greek philosophic deity, he never lost the personal and merciful God of the Jews." There are many passages in Philo where Yahweh appears quite unlike the Existent. In this, Philo is like the countless generations after him who would "philosophize about the Absolute but pray to God the Father." It is Goodenough's belief that Philo "does come nearer to calling the mystical apprehension the 'higher' apprehension than he does the Jewish."[20] ("Mystical" here means the results of metaphysical speculation.)

> But the fact was that as a Jew and a man of everyday experience, he needed the personal loving God, and as a thinker and mystic he needed the other. He did not give up one for the other, and apparently had no notion of their incompatibility. He would have been highly anachronistic had he done so. The whole question of 'personality' in God had not been raised by either Jew or Greek, and it never entered Philo's head to raise it. The matter had reached only the stage of questioning 'anthropomorphisms' and here Philo stands firmly with the Greek philosophers, to the point of saying that the anthropomorphic passages in the Bible are nonsense if taken literally.[21]

Gutmann, writing about Philo in the context of the history of Jewish philosophy, characterizes Philo as one who replaced Jewish ideas with Greek ones. With reference to God, to the extent that Philo insists on the transcendence of God, Jewish ideas are present. But it is Gutmann's opinion that this transcendence arises rather in opposition to Stoic materialism than out of Philo's own concept of a personal God, which latter conception Gutmann says is completely missing in Philo. "If he [Philo] occasionally seems to approach the biblical conception of a personal God, this may more safely be considered inconsistency rather than the essential nature of his teaching"![22] This is a bit strong, and most authors would not go that far. It does show, however, what an impersonal idea of God one can obtain from reading Philo. Gutmann also admits the personal element:

The two sides of Philo's religious consciousness are reflected also in his theological speculation. His concept of God, which is above and beyond all positive content, corresponds to the mystical. There is no doubt that for Philo, this idea of God is ultimately the valid one; the personal traits occasionally attributed to God are, from a philosophic point of view, inconsequential lapses from consistency. However, what appears as mere inconsistency from a theoretical point of view, may well be an essential part in the religious context of Philo's thought. Despite the fact that the purely abstract idea of God logically excludes a personalistic conception, Philo seems unable to do without the latter when he wants to say what God really means for him.[23]

In Philo we see very clearly the dynamic pointed out by Murray, that is the transition from speaking about the God-as-he-is-for-me to the God-as-he-is-in-himself. This can be seen especially in Philo's treatment of the "otherness" of God.

In the scriptures God is certainly "other," not like man, transcendent. This is how he appears when man stands in his presence. When we say, from our experience, that God is "other," that does not tell us of what his otherness consists. Philosophy tries to tell us. In Philo we see how God's "otherness," a scriptural intuition, becomes God's "immateriality" and "incorporeality."

Wolfson says that it was Philo who turned the otherness of the God of Israel into the incorporeality of God; Philo then applied to God all the *attributes* of incorporeality, the absence of passions among them.

What Philo means to say...is that the scriptural doctrine of the unlikeness of God rests upon the philosophical doctrine of the incorporeality of God. 'Unlikeness' thus with him becomes 'incorporeality' and the denial of the likeness of God to any other being comes to mean with him the exclusion from God's nature of anything that may, however indirectly, imply corporeality, so that God, he says, not only has no body or bodily organs or sense-perception but also no such human emotions as jealousy, wrath, and anger.[24]

This seems to be another instance of where the philosophical truth takes precedence over the biblical. Philosophy knows of spiritual and material realities, and assigns certain properties to each. For the philosophy of the time, the spiritual world shared in the properties of the immovable, eternal ideas. Philo, says Wolfson, made God into the likeness of an idea.[25] Are God's qualities more akin to the vision of the "soul-lovers, or the body-lovers" (to use Philo's own words)? I would say both, each in its own way.

According to Wolfson, Philo also goes beyond both Plato and Aristotle in the matter of the knowability of God. Neither Plato nor Aristotle ever said that God could not be defined or known. This conception of the ineffability or unnameability of God is not found in any other Greek philosopher before Philo. This point is mentioned here to emphasize the extreme extent of Philo's philosophical transcendence. It is possible to conjecture that the religious sense of God's otherness, which was his Jewish heritage, pushed his philosophical speculations to their furthest limits.

We come, finally, to Philo's specific answer to the problem of anthropomorphisms in the Bible. It is not a new problem in Judaism but part and parcel of the ongoing interpretation of the Word of God. God is other, not like a man. But this God is spoken of in anthropomorphic terms. He is different, and also somehow "like" man. How to reconcile these two notions?

The general solution of the rabbis was to say that such expressions are not to be taken literally; secondly, such words are used so that they may be useful in teaching the people. Philo accepted both of these approaches, but he comes up with yet a third: philosophical allegory. "Powers" is another name Philo uses for the anthropomorphisms in the Bible. He speaks of the "many-named powers." For Philo, God really has only one property, and that is activity: God is ever-active. Thus, when Philo speaks of even the unchangeableness of God, he means that God is unchanging in his being constantly active. It is important to emphasize this: for God to be unchanging means that he is ever active.

A further point: it is the property of everything created to "suffer action": "It is the property of God to act [and]...the property of the created to suffer action."[26] And now, (the crux of the matter) between these two—the creator and the created, the active and the passive—there can be no reciprocal relationship. Philo states what shall become the traditional answer in Western philosophy; it remains largely the answer today:[27]

> For the Existant considered as existent is not relative; He is full of himself and He is sufficient for himself. It was so before the creation of the world, and is equally so after the creation of all that is. He cannot change nor alter and needs nothing else at all, so that all things are His but He himself in the proper sense belongs to none.[28]

Philo, it seems, is the first theologian of note to fall into the fallacy which Gollwitzer mentioned,[29] the fallacy of supposing that philosophical terms are less anthropomorphic or more accurate than biblical terms in describing the reality of God. Philo's error, of which in some ways we are the inheritors, was to suppose that the abstract notion of God was the "real" truth behind the biblical. Philo did the "one thing" which believers ought not to do: make any other title (word, name) for God subordinate to Yahweh. To quote Gollwitzer again, "Yahweh is the meaning of the symbolic word 'God' as the Bible understands it."

A great deal more could be said of this fascinating man Philo, but this suffices for our purposes. Philo is *the* representative of Hellenistic Judaism which played such a prominent role in forging the Christian doctrine of God. Many of the problems which faced the Christian thinkers had already been confronted and solved by Philo in his own way. The Christian writers in many areas were his heirs, and certainly in this area of the transcendence of God.

7. The Impassible

Wait for him who is above time—the Timeless, the Invisible, who for our sake became visible, the Impassible, who became subject to suffering on our account and for our sake endured everything.

St. Ignatius of Antioch, Poly. 3, 2

[In the Incarnation]...the invisible was made visible, and the incomprehensible comprehensible, and the impassible passible.

St. Irenaeus of Lyon, *Adversus Haereses*, III, 17, 6

The identification of the God of the philosophers with the God of the Bible [was] later taken over by the Christian apologists and the early Church fathers.

Martin Hengel, *Judaism and Hellenism*

The doctrine of divine impassibility proved a particularly troublesome one for the fathers partly because it had to be maintained alongside the Old Testament picture of a wrathful, angry, repentant, merciful God, but mainly...because the very thrust of the revelation in Jesus Christ was that God saves the world by suffering in and with the world. The apparent Biblical attribution of suffering to incarnate deity was understood by the fathers as a Christological problem and it was met there by attributing the suffering of Christ to the human nature. The Biblical language was explained away by allegorical exegesis.

Burton Cooper, *The Idea of God*

In Chapter Five we saw that the biblical, relational God of the Old Testament was very much the God of Jesus. We also saw that despite the NT use of some philosophical phrases and terms, these latter were wholly subjected to the intuitions of the faith. Then, in the preceding Chapter, we looked into the world of Hellenistic Judiasm, that current of thought which had a profound influence on Christian doctrine.

We are now going to attempt to show how the early Christian writers, influenced by the Greek philosophical tradition, began to speak about God in a very unscriptural fashion. Many of these writers were non-Jews and Greek-educated. If it is an exaggeration to speak of an "Hellenization of Christianity" in their writings, implying that the Christian faith became something other than it originally was, I think it correct to say that *in some points of the Fathers' theology* the result was inadequate and reflected a certain Hellenization of the faith. I believe one of the inadequacies concerned the pathos of God.

Because of the platonic atmosphere, because most of the debates centered around God's transcendence and his relation to the cosmos, God the Father became more and more the Unapproachable One, the Impassible One, while the God-Man Jesus served the purposes of a personal, relational God. Thus the living, relational, involved Yahweh of the Old Testament did not become more remote because of the Incarnation. Jesus became the "passible" God to fulfill the real religious needs of the Christian; the Father became impassible and remote to some extent, to fulfill the current philosophical exegencies of the times and to satisfy both the critics and the intellectual adherents of the new religion.

By looking into the mental world of Philo we acquired some notion of the impact of philosophical thought on a believing Jew. We will not enter so deeply into any of the thought of the writers in this early period because in the history of thought they are not of Philo's stature. It is not until we come to Clement of Alexandria (Chapter Eight) that we find a Christian who both knew the Greek philosophical tradition and was able to strive for a conscious synthesis between it and the Christian message.

A helpful approach to the post-New Testament world would be to get a general idea of the philosophical atmosphere as regards questions of God, man and the world. Again, we leave it to the experts to make all the fine distinctions and connections between these writers and their contemporary mentors. What we are interested in here is a general feeling of the philosophical climate of the times. For the following section we are much indebted to Norris' important book.

The Christians had to learn the language and thought forms of Greek philosophy in order to carry on an intellectual dialogue with non-Christians who challenged the former's faith. Thus, these early Christian writers tried to do for Christianity what Philo had tried to do for Judaism: show how their religion complements or corresponds or differs from the philosophical wisdom of the Greeks. "It was necessary to show how the basic principles of biblical faith could be made comprehensible in terms of the ideas and values which went together to make up the Hellenistic picture."[1]

The Hellenistic world picture was basically Platonic, although it is well known that there were a variety of interpretations of Plato. Middle Platonism, as it was called, was the school which most influenced the Christians of the second century. This was one variation of Plato's basic scheme, but the basic scheme was all pervasive.

What was the basic scheme? There were two levels of reality. The physical world was the world of becoming. It was inferior because ever subject to the law of change; it was always becoming something else. Thus, it could offer no basis for reliable knowledge.

Then there was the intelligible world of being. This was grasped with the mind alone. "The truth of things is the immaterial Pattern which reason grasps, not the distorted and unstable shadow which the eye sees."[2] Ideas are the genuinely real because they are eternal and do not change. The "divine" is anything which participates in Being as opposed to Becoming. Thus, man's true destiny is to delight in contemplation of Being in contrast to the order of Becoming, that is, in ideas of the mind rather than in things of the world as we see them.

This contrast and scheme carried through to all aspects of reality: Becoming is unreal; only Being is the truly real. "The outcome of this dichotomized epistemology is the theory of two worlds corresponding to different ways of knowing. One is a world of pure reality, immune to change; the other is a world of relative actuality, characterized by coming and passing away. One world is and never becomes; the other becomes and never is."[3]

In this view, "eternal truths are arrived at conceptually, not perceptually."[4] What we see is not really what things are. They really are something else. We cannot take our truth about reality from our eyes and our ears, from our senses. We must get behind them to discover their true nature. "These ideas were to become, in ever changing form, part of the common religious heritage of the world into which Christianity came."[5]

For the Greek, the world has a natural order which does not change. It is constituted by an eternal order "which does not change in structure even though the things and events in which this order is realized are in constant process of alteration."[6]

For the Hebrew, on the other hand, the world is not an eternally fixed pattern. It is more like a stage on which a drama is taking place. The meaning is in the developing story. "The world is a complex tapestry of human life and human decision, viewed in historical perspective and evaluated in terms of its correspondence with a divine will which inexorably seeks fulfillment of its purposes."[7]

As already mentioned, for the Greeks, the "divine" stands for a *type* of thing which is characterized by rationality, stability and permanence: "Greek theology tends to use the word 'God' to refer to a universal principle of explanation, a pre-supposition of the world order viewed as a natural system."[8] The Hebrews also used the word "God," but instead of developing a rational theology, they fashioned, in keeping with a peculiar sense of perception, a theology of historical experience.

The God which the Christians inherited from Israel was not a "kind of reality" which shared in the properties of the ideal world; nor was he a "principle of universal explanation." He was Yahweh, the God who is known by what he does. He was Yahweh, the dynamic, intensely personal God who guides and directs the history of his people, nay, is intimately bound up in some way with it. "The Greek deity is the final point of stability in a world of apparently senseless change. The Hebrew Lord is the initiator of significant change which transforms the character of historical experience. As such, he, like the events through which he is known, has a specific character. Hence, in the final instance he is named, not defined; and as the Lord of world history he is unique."[9]

There is one more concept (indeed, for this study the *central concept*) connected with this Platonic world view that is very pertinent to our topic. It is the notion of *apatheia*, the technical Greek word for "impassible."

In the period we are considering, the word had several connotations. In a strictly *physical* sense, it certainly did mean unchangeableness—"incapable of being affected by outside influences, incapable of feeling..." However, in its *ethical* sense, it meant a being that was truly *free*:

> Originally it [*apatheia*] did not mean the petrification of men, nor does it denote those symptoms of illness which are today described as apathy, indifference, and alienation. Rather it denotes the freedom of man and his superiority to the world

in corresponding to the perfect, all-sufficient freedom of the Godhead. The apathetic God could therefore be understood as the free God who freed others for himself.[10]

But this word was a two-edged sword, because its opposite—pathos—*was connected with dependence on the lower passions, drives and compulsions.* To be controlled by such motions was considered an imperfect state. The goal was perfect freedom—apatheia—but this word also connoted an incapacity to be affected by any outside influence. We will see that by the time of Clement of Alexandria the word carried this latter meaning, so much so that Clement could write about Jesus himself: "He was altogether impassible, into Him no movements of passion could find their way, neither pleasure nor pain."

Thus, when the Christian writers of the second century begin to call God *apatheis*, that kind of God is now totally unaffected by any outside influence of the world or man. The two words *pathos* and *apatheia* exclude one another, and this facile and superficial distinction was applied to the infinitely complex reality of God. Did they ever ask the question of whether God is in some respects passible and in some respects impassible? This is the question being asked in recent times; it is a question which might have been well-nigh impossible to ask in the second century.

With all this background in mind now—left and right hemispheres of the brain, Greek and Hebrew thought-patterns, the biblical idea of God, Philo and the contribution of Hellenistic Judaism, the general philosophical climate of the second century—we would like to take a look at some of the Christian writers of the second century, the century which laid the groundwork for the Christian doctrine of God.

It is the century of the Apostolic Fathers, of the Greek apologists, of Irenaeus, Clement of Alexandria, and the great Origen. Again, a survey will be sufficient, because

I believe that, just as in the Bible, so here too, the main lines are clear; further in-depth study would only put more flesh on what are clearly discernible aspects of the doctrine of God.

The two indisputable tenets of faith in the NT are 1) that the Cross of Jesus is at the heart of man's redemption, and 2) that this Jesus is the Son of God come in the flesh. It is Mozley's opinion that concentrated emphasis on these two convictions was only partially carried forward into the second century.[11] The writers we are going to consider during the rest of this book convey a picture of their intellectual struggle between the transcendence of God, his otherness, and the Incarnation, the coming in the flesh of this God and his real suffering for man.

We will first look briefly at Ignatius of Antioch. He was the most well-known and the most widely read of the Apostolic Fathers, a title given to Christian writers who were considered to be in close proximity, both in time and mentality, to the Apostolic age. Their writings, therefore, are pastoral, designed to exhort, instruct and inspire; they are not consciously philosophical or "intellectual." For our purposes, this latter point is significant.

Ignatius, the third bishop of Antioch, was also called Theophorus, a Greek name. Antioch was a cosmopolitan city and perhaps the first place where Christians came into real contact with the Greek world and culture. We know that some of the early Christians went there after the fall of Jerusalem, and that in Antioch they first received the name of Christians (Ac 11:26). It is possible also that in this city Hellenistic notions first began to color the message of the NT.

Tixeront says of Ignatius, "It is surmised that he was born a pagan and became converted to the faith later in life."[12] These facts are important. We begin to have Christians with no real Jewish tradition and culture—no Hebrew mind—who see the teachings of Christianity through different eyes. In this situation, even if similar words are used, i.e., "God," it is no longer exactly Yahweh or the Father of Our Lord Jesus.

It is in Ignatius' letters that we find the word *apatheis* in Christian literature for the first time. (It will be recalled that this technical Greek word for impassible does not appear in scripture.) Robert Grant says that Ignatius' writings are very important because they portray some kind of *tradition* of philosophical reflection.

In the passage we quoted at the beginning of this chapter, Ignatius says: "[Jesus Christ] the eternal; the invisible, visible for us; the intangible; the impassible, passible for us; the one who endured for us in every way" (Poly. 3, 2). Grant says that in this passage a *third stage* of reflection is evident. Since these epithets of the negative theology—invisible, intangible, impassible—are applied to both God the Father *and* Christ, there must have been a stage when they were first applied to the Father and then also to Christ. "These paradoxes," says Grant, "come from a combination of language about God with language about Christ's passion."[13]

What we see in conflict now are Greek notions about God clashing with the reality of the Incarnation. The two notions, as they stand, are incompatible. All Ignatius can do is say them together and hold them in paradoxical tension. (One can only fondly speculate what the outcome would have been if at this point in Christian history some great Jewish rabbi of the anthropomorphic school had become a convert and laid the theological foundations using the rabbinic traditions.)

It is quite clear in Ignatius that for him the Deity itself is impassible: "Christ in the incarnate state becomes voluntarily subject to certain conditions which were *wholly absent till then*" (italics mine).[14] "This balanced, antithetical statement shows that we must not attribute to him [Ignatius] views of a suffering God outside of the sphere of the Incarnation."[15] Thus one of the first crucial (and it might be added, philosophically naive) steps is taken by a Christian writer to use philosophical terminology concerning the mystery of the Godhead and the Incarnation. All Ignatius can do is state the dilemma: the Impassible has become passible. He does not attempt to go any further. His ideas tend in one direction while his heart cries "suffer me to follow the example of the passion of my God" (*Ad Rm* 6).

Early Christianity, as we mentioned briefly in the first chapter, was quite uncritical about its doctrine of God. Jewish converts from Palestine had a wealth of devotional knowledge about God, and they saw Jesus as the fulfillment of their ancient faith. Greek converts acquired many of their notions from the synagogues of the dispersion, in places such as Antioch and Alexandria.

Thus, in a city like Antioch, a seaport exposed to all the currents of the day, there would have been a potpourri of devotional and loose philosophical phrases circulating about the nature of the Deity. To continue the quotation from Goodenough cited in the first chapter:

> When Christianity was attacked by Jews or pagans, recourse was had of necessity to the philosophical terminology, which was then brought forward with more confidence than understanding, and given an emphasis utterly disproportionate to its real significance for their Faith. Naturally in such a case the terminology shows no sign of having been applied with careful eye to consistency or appropriateness.[16]

This observation was written over fifty years ago, but it is confirmed by present-day scholars: In the New Testament and the Apostolic Fathers there is no conscious dialogue taking place between faith and philosophy. There is only a "natural, instinctive, and unsystematic appropriation of certain of the intellectual resources of... Hellenistic Judaism in particular."[17]

This fact of the "unsystematic appropriation" of notions about God on the part of these early writers is extremely important for our study; it is especially important for the rethinking of questions from the dogmatic point of view. If the question was never seriously asked concerning the Father's passibility, or if the question was never critically examined, then statements cannot be taken to "prove" such a position, except, perhaps, as witnesses to a certain emphasis or tendency. The uncritical nature of the statements of this period will be worth emphasizing.

Pollard thanks Dr. D. M. Baille for this insight: "The idea of impassibility appeared in some of the earliest post-apostolic writings of the Church; it is a position which is assumed rather than argued for."[18] "The Fathers accepted the negative Hellenic interpretation of change and they affirmed the concept of divine absoluteness because it had the virtue of excluding by definition all elements of change in the divine being. It is worth stressing that the fathers *presupposed* (ital. mine) God's absoluteness in all aspects of his being with neither qualification nor exception."[19] God's "absolute impassibility" was part of this absoluteness.

We have already quoted Goodenough to the effect that Greek Jews "would have only understood the Jewish God of Abraham, while they would have used the philosophical phrases of the learned with the indiscrimination of unintelligence."[20] This is true for most people. Very few are capable of thinking out for themselves all the implications and underpinnings of the words they use about God. Would not this also apply to convert-bishops of the second century? Phrases about God were part of the terminology of the day. They were used, not in a technical, but in a popular fashion.

"We should not claim," says Grant, "that the specific doctrines of ancient theologians are permanently valid. All we should claim is that the approach which early fathers used is still significant."[21] This is not, of course, a denial of tradition, that in some way it is a permanently valid criterion. He simply means that the use of philosophy to defend and elaborate the data of revelation is an ongoing process. All the specific details of doctrines worked out centuries ago are subject to reinterpretation and revision.

There was another group of writers and thinkers in the second century whom we call "apologists." They were Christians who tried, on a more intellectual, philosophical level, to answer the objections of the intelligentsia. They tried to give a reason for the faith that was in them (1 Pt 3:15). Justin Martyr was the most famous and influential.

Justin is something of a Christian Philo, though lacking his Jewish background. Justin shares the latter's attitude toward Greek philosophy and his attempt to keep the faith as the ultimate criterion. Justin took the Greek philosophers seriously, and saw similarities between their words and the words of scripture. The Greek philosophers, Justin says, had a share in the Logos, and the Logos is Christ. Christ is the fullness of what the philosophers had only in part.

For Justin, philosophy is "a religious search for the vision of God."[22] In many ways, philosophy had become a substitute for religion for many who were searching for wisdom during this second century. Justin tells us that he came to Christianity through his philosophical quest. We mention here only certain aspects of his doctrine of God.

> Justin's assertions of the transcendence, ineffability, and immutability of God place him quite in line with the Platonic tendency to define God in terms of contrast with the world and with man as, when extended to their furthest point, lead to a series of negations and the complete absence of positive descriptions. That God is *atreptos*, unchangeable, is a conviction common to him and to those for whom he writes.[23]

Justin's God is the "Craftsman" of Middle Platonism. It was a conception of Deity which seemed to Justin to correspond in many ways to the God of the scriptures. It was common for contemporary pagan philosophers like Albinus to apply to God epithets such as ingenerate, incomprehensible, indivisible and immortal. By these terms, men like Albinus attempted to specify the difference between the universe and the Reality which is no part of the universe.[24] Nothing seemed more natural and right to Justin than to appropriate this language to express the God of the Bible.

> The biblical sense of God's 'beyondness' Justin tried to capture by use of the same language which he employs to affirm the ultimacy of God. Words like 'ingenerate' and 'impassible' set God over against the world by making implicit use of the Platonic distinction between Being—or the Source of Being—and Becoming. God is the apex of the eternal and changeless order of intelligible reality; and as such he is 'beyond' the mutable and perishable world which is his creation.[25]
>
> Justin does not, however, perceive that his appropriation of the negative language of Middle Platonism theology conceals an ambiguity and a problem. 'Being' and 'Becoming'—or 'ingenerate' and 'generate'—denote, in a Platonic system, logical contraries, that is, loosely speaking, they stand for opposed qualities within a single 'spectrum.' Consequently, the realities which they name *exclude* each other; and God's transcendence over the world, when figured in terms of the contrast between Being and Becoming, turns out to be a form of necessary separation from the world.[26]
>
> Almost thoughtlessly, Justin dresses this Deity in the attributes of the scriptural God.[27]

The process which takes place in Justin's mind is easy to understand. He does not know the Yahweh of the bible too well, being a convert from paganism. Through his faith he comes to know that God is the One God, wholly transcendent, wholly Other. Justin then proceeds to clothe God with all the transcendent qualities of the world of Being which have been worked out by the Greek platonic mind.

In Justin, God acquires more and more the qualities of the intellect (Greek, left hemisphere), while the personal, related God of the Hebrews becomes more and more cut off from his creation. The angry, jealous, compassionate Yahweh evolves, in Justin's thought, into Being. Instead of a God with whom someone struggles and wrestles and argues, God becomes a simple object of contemplation: "Being, in a Platonic system, represents a static Object of contemplation and desire. Set apart from the visible order, it influences the world because it is the vision which fills the mind and directs the activity of the soul."[28] (Like a magnet in a swivel chair, as someone once described it!) It is clear that Justin now gives a more intellectually sophisticated basis to the impassibility of God, a basis it did not have in the uncritical works of the Apostolic Fathers.

The other apologists are in the same tradition. Tatian (b. circa 120) was from Assyria, a disciple of Justin, and he eventually left the orthodox Church. As regards the impassibility of God, "the doctrine of Tatian points in the same direction as that of Justin."[29] In at least one passage, Tatian speaks of the holy Spirit as "the minister of the suffering God" (Oratio 13).

Theophilus of Antioch was the seventh bishop of that city from about 169 to 180 A.D., and he is a very interesting thinker in regard to our question. He was born near the Euphrates and therefore would have been influenced by Mesopotamian ways. Though Greek-educated, he also knew Hebrew. His thinking on the pathos of God reflects both attitudes. If a theology of the pathos of God were being attempted, his writings would serve as a fruitful area of study from the traditional standpoint.

He writes in one of his treatises: "Is God angry? Yes, He is angry with those who act wickedly, but He is good and kind and merciful to those who love and fear Him. . ." (Ad Autoly. 1, 3). Then, just a few lines later, he writes: "And He [God] is without beginning, because He is unbegotten; and He is unchangeable, because He is immortal" (1, 4). Mozley has some pertinent comments on this sequence of ideas in Theophilus:

> When Theophilus goes on almost immediately to say that God is 'unchangeable, inasmuch as He is immortal,' we must regard him as meaning that no outside force can so act upon God as to alter the essential constancy of His nature. In this sense he could have used of God, as Justin did, the adjective *apathes*, but (this) Stoic idea of a God who is above all feeling would be incompatible with what he had already said [v.g., about God's anger].[30]

Theophilus from Syria was enough of a Semite not to make God completely unfeeling.

This same ambiguity, which has remained in the Christian doctrine of God to the present time, is clearly evidenced by another of the apologists, Athenagoras of Athens. According to tradition he was from Alexandria, was well versed in Greek philosophy, and wrote the first rational proof to justify the Christian doctrine of the unity of God.

He, too, is caught up in his Apology (177 A.D.) in the fashionable pastime of getting the Greek gods in order. All anthropomorphisms must be abolished: "There is neither anger, nor desire and appetite, nor procreative seed, in gods...for I call even men rude and stupid who give way to anger and grief" (Apology, 21). The whole passage is a dehumanizing of the Greek gods, especially as regards their emotional and changeable aspects.

In an earlier passage on the unity of the true God, Athenagoras had described Him as "uncreated and impassible and indivisible" (8). Then he says: "If we satisfied ourselves with advancing such considerations as these [scil. purely rational considerations], our doctrines might by some be looked upon as human. But, since the voice of the prophets confirm our arguments..." (9). He then brings forth several texts from scripture to prove especially that God is one: "The Lord is our God; no other can be compared with him" (Is 41:4); "Before me there was no other God, and after me there shall be none; I am God and there is none besides Me" (Is 43:10).

One would expect him to quote some texts concerning the other aspects mentioned, such as impassibility —but there are none; Athenagoras goes on to something else. He said he was going to turn to the prophets. Is it possible that he could not find the impassible God there? He had said earlier that Christians have another source of knowledge besides reason, i.e., the prophetic spirit: "But we have for witnesses of the things we apprehend and believe, prophets, men who have pronounced concerning God and the things of God, guided by the Spirit of God" (VIII). Then, curiously, in his passage on the Trinity, he makes this opening remark:

> But we are not atheists, therefore, seeing that we acknowledge one God, uncreated, eternal, invisible, impassible, incomprehensible, illimitable, who is apprehended by the understanding only and the reason...I have sufficiently demonstrated. (X)

Here the philosopher's true bias is revealed: "apprehended by the understanding alone." Rational knowledge takes precedence over the prophetic. Tradition has it that Athenagoras was the first master of the catechetical school in Alexandria. In subsequent decades the same milieu would host Clement and Origen.

St. Irenaeus of Lyons (140-202) was the outstanding defender of the Faith in the second century. He has been called the Father of Orthodoxy, especially because of his work *Against Heresies*.[32] He was the champion of the real suffering of Jesus. (We have already seen that a contemporary, Clement of Alexandria, was not altogether clear on this point.) Concerning the heretics and their teaching about Jesus, Irenaeus writes:

> They say that after his baptism, Christ descended upon him [Jesus] in the form of a dove from the Supreme Ruler, and

> that then he proclaimed the unknown Father, and performed miracles. But at last Christ departed from Jesus, and then Jesus suffered and rose again, while Christ remained impassible, inasmuch as he was a spiritual being. I,xxvi,i (Also, cf. III,xi,3,7)

For someone unfamiliar with the Gnostics of the second century, this may seem like a very bizarre doctrine. It surely was. They postulated two beings, Jesus and Christ. They wished to safeguard the "divineness" of Christ the Savior, so they had him coming and going upon the man Jesus, avoiding undignified moments such as birth, suffering and death.

Irenaeus champions the true suffering of Jesus Christ the Savior. Unequivocally and often with great beauty he states many times the tradition from the Apostles:

> Thus the apostles did not preach another God, or another Fullness; nor that the Christ who suffered and rose again was one, while he who flew off on high was another, and remained impassible. III,xii,4 2
>
> Thus the apostles did not change God, but preached to the people that Christ was Jesus the crucified one, whom the same God that had sent the prophets, being God Himself, raised up, and gave in Him salvation to men. III,xii,4
>
> This is the mystery which he [Paul] says was made known to him by revelation, that He who suffered under Pontius Pilate, the same is Lord of all, and King, and God, and Judge.... III,xii,8

That Irenaeus believed in and taught the real suffering of Jesus is beyond doubt; it is part of our Christian faith. It is also beyond doubt that Irenaeus believed in the impassibility of God. When proving the former doctrine, he quotes the scriptures; when speaking about the latter,

> [Irenaeus] himself asserts in many ways the divine transcendence. 'God needs nothing and is self-sufficient' (III,viii,3). 'Man cannot serve him as to add anything to Him'

(IV,xxv,1); 'the invisible was made visible, and the incomprehensible comprehensible, and the impassible passible' (III,xvii,7). It never occurred to Irenaeus to look for any archtype of human passibility in the divine nature.[33]

Irenaeus was not a philosopher, and generally he mistrusted philosophical speculation. Yet, when he comes to "prove" God's impassibility, the words he uses are from philosophy not scripture. Furthermore, they are used quite uncritically, indicating that he is very much dependent on the tradition gone before him.

> Irenaeus, in his campaign against the Gnostics, makes use of exegetical and theological ideas which he had inherited from previous Christian writers, and from the Apologists in particular. Through these sources, if not directly, his understanding of the Scriptures is affected in a real measure by commonplace conceptions whose roots lie in the Greek philosophical tradition....[34]

That the Impassible became passible expresses exactly the Christian dilemma in the second century. Irenaeus' genius lies in holding to the real suffering of Christ despite his belief in the impassibility of God. God is close to man, and the Incarnation effects a still closer union. But for Ireneaus it is clear that impassibility is an essential characteristic of the divine nature. He proclaimed the reality of Christ's life and sufferings for man, but left unresolved the problem of impassibility in relation to Jesus.

One of the curious features of the debate with the Gnostics on this point was that they believed very much in some measure of suffering in their Eons, spiritual beings who had emanated from the ultimate Bythus. "Irenaeus considered that the logic of the [Gnostics] involved the doctrine of a finite and changeable God,"[34] and he fought them on this front also. In other words, the Gnostics believed in some kind of pathos in their Eons but would not allow suffering in Christ the Savior; Irenaeus, on the other hand, emphatically taught the real suffering of the Christ, but denied any kind of suffering in the Deity as such:

> In his [Irenaeus'] theology God seems less aloof in his transcendence. Morally and spiritually He is portrayed as more akin to man. The Incarnation effects the closest union of Him with men. But that impassibility is for him an essential attribute of the divine nature, we cannot doubt.35

The Gnostics were Christians, albeit heretical ones. It should be noted, however, that they were able to reconcile the notion of passion with beings in the "spiritual sphere." It seems that the religious intuition of a large number of people included this feature. It is clear from our faith that Jesus really suffered. Is it also "of faith" that God is impassible? Irenaeus thought so, and such was his teaching. The decisive step had been taken: It was the *Impassible* who became passible.

8. The Unknowable

If, then, abstracting all that belongs to bodies and things called incorporeal, we cast ourselves into the greatness of Christ, and thence advance into immensity by holiness, we may reach somehow to the conception of the Almighty, knowing not what He is, but what He is not. And form and motion, or standing, or a throne, or place, or right hand, or left, are not at all to be conceived as belonging to the Father of the universe, although it is so written. The First Cause is not then in space, but above both space, and time, and name, and conception.

Clement of Alexandria, *The Stromata*, V,xi

The doctrines to which Clement resorts in order to describe the transcendence of God occur also in Philo, in the Platonic tradition, and in the Gnostic systems of the second century A.D., and go back ultimately to some passages of Plato. Particularly important is the doctrine of the absolute unknowability of the first principle.

Salvatore R. C. Lilla, *Clement of Alexandria*

Thought is abstract; the intolerant use of abstractions is the major vice of the intellect.

A. N. Whitehead, *Science and the Modern World*

But the Lord did not say that both the Father and the Son could not be known at all (*in totum*), for in that case His advent would have been superfluous. For why did He come hither? Was it that He should say to us, 'Never mind seeking after God; for He is unknown, and ye shall not find Him.' The

Lord taught us that no man is capable of knowing God unless he be taught of God; that is, God cannot be known without God: but this is the express will of the Father, that God should be known. For they shall know Him to whomsoever the Son has revealed Him.

Irenaeus of Lyons, *Against Heresies*, IV,vi,4

Before Clement of Alexandria (150-215) the use of explicit philosophical language by Christian writers was either unconscious and quite uncritical (as in the Apostolic Fathers), or in its early, almost amateurish stages, as in Justin and Irenaeus. Clement, on the other hand, born probably in Athens, is a Hellenistic philosopher to the core of his soul. He was educated in the classical schools and came to Christianity through a philosophical search for the truth. He was a convert, lacking knowledge of the Hebrew tradition and ways.

It is not possible to overestimate the importance of Clement for Christian theology. Whereas Christian teachers up to this time had mainly relied on oral teaching, Clement adds the written page as a means of transmitting the truth. And he gives this truth a consciously scientific exposition, trying to show the relationship between philosophy, Christianity and contemporary thought. "He was the first to expand, with a moral and pedagogical purpose, the relations of philosophy and theology, and it was due in great measure to him that Alexandria became a first-class centre of influence in the East eclipsing the Churches of Asia and Syria. Clement was a pioneer in theology...."[1] "In some sense...Clement may be seen as the founder of theology...he was the first, so far as we can tell, to transfer to Christianity, in his quest for an understanding of the faith, the language and spirit of philosophical knowledge."[2]

It is because of these facts that the present study will end with Clement. The crucial decisions as regards the transcendence, and hence the impassibility of God were made by Philo, and then, consciously or unconsciously, by the Christian writers who followed him.

Clement thought of himself as quite orthodox; he also knew that there were many areas of teaching still open for debate. In his most famous work, *The Stromata*, he does not hesitate to sow the seeds of a great variety of ideas. But we cannot doubt that he believed his teaching on the main doctrines of the faith to be fully in keeping with the traditions of the Fathers.

Clement believed just as strongly in the truth of the Greek philosophical tradition, which he saw (as did Philo and Justin before him) as a kind of natural preparation for the revelation of God in the scriptures. He gives arguments for his positions from the Greek tradition and from the scriptures. Nor is this a mere conformism or a superficial desire to conciliate all sides. It flowed from deep convictions: "For him [Clement] there is no irreconcilable antithesis between the two. The classical philosophers and the 'barbaric' prophets of the Old Testament seem to stand almost completely in line with one another as pioneers of the truth which was revealed in Christ."[3] "He undertook to combine with ecclesiastical tradition elements that are foreign to it. He borrowed from Greek philosophy, especially Plato, and held that as the Jews were led to Christianity through the Old Testament, the Gentiles should come through philosophy."[4]

Salvatore Lilla has written one of the major studies on Clement of Alexandria. He concludes that Clement goes beyond merely using philosophy to better clarify the truths of the faith. In some real sense, Clement saw Greek philosophy as a way of saying the *same thing in different words*:

> Clement's use of Greek philosophical doctrines goes far beyond the borrowing of some terms which do not influence his Christianity at all and which represent only a superficial tinge: ...in theology Clement has produced a process of

Hellenization of Christianity which is closely parallel to the process of Hellenization of Judaism which is characteristic of Philo's work. Clement does not borrow a few doctrines or 'terms' of Greek philosophy simply because he wants to speak with the heathen philosophers in their own language in order to convert them to his own religion....[he] considered the best doctrines of Greek philosophy as practically one and the same thing with the highest aspect of Christianity, since they, according to him, had been originated by the divine Logos.[5]

In Clement's view the image of God is in every man. Therefore, the reasonings of philosophy are also in some way God-given, and should be appreciated by Christians. Reason and revelation cooperate just as do freedom of the human will and divine grace. "To deny that Philosophy is God's gift is to deny providence and the image of God in creation. Clement has high hopes for the salvation of Greek sages. God's saving purpose is not confined to his covenant with the Hebrews."[6] "Both the Old Testament and Greek philosophy are alike tutors to bring us to Christ and are both tributaries of the one great river of Christianity. In Christ, Clement possesses the full truth only partially apprehended by the different schools, each of which has discovered some element of the truth."[7]

We spent so much time on Philo in Chapter Six because Clement was heavily dependent on him and simply accepted many of the conclusions that Philo had arrived at. Clement is more accepting of Platonism than Philo was "and thinks of many Platonic doctrines as coming to him with Biblical authority to support them."[8] It will become clear from what follows that the impassibility of God was one of these doctrines that Clement accepted from Philo as being a part of the biblical revelation.

Clement, like Philo, tends to interpret scripture in the light of philosophy and vice versa. For example, "[Plato] had heard right well that the all-wise Moses, ascending the mount for holy contemplation, to the summit of intellectual objects..." (*Stromata*, V,xii). What is Moses doing on Sinai? He is contemplating the eternal ideas of Greek metaphysics!

This method of interpreting scripture is extremely important for our present study. The method comes from Philo and "is based on Philo's conception of the relationship between philosophy and theology or wisdom as well as the tendency of the Jewish author to interpret the Old Testament in terms of Greek philosophy."[9] "Very useful," says Clement himself, "is the mode of symbolic interpretation for many purposes; and it is helpful to the right theology, and to piety, and to the display of intelligence, and the practise of brevity, and the exhibition of wisdom" (*Stromata*, V,viii).

All these principles then—that revelation and philosophy both proceed from the Logos, that there is a hidden meaning to scripture to be explained by allegory— are functioning in Clement's approach to the interpretation of the Scriptures and the elucidation of the truths of Christianity. He was a dyed-in-the-wool Greek philosopher converted to Christianity, and teaching and studying in a city saturated with Hellenistic Judaism, Platonism, and Gnosticism. Given this background, (and keeping in mind the general trend in the second century toward an extreme approach to God's transcendence) we will be in a good position to consider Clement's doctrine of God. The school which Clement helped to foster had an aversion for the emotional elements of life as representing the irrational side of man. The *"via negativa"* was the preferred means of speaking about God. All these factors combine "to enlist its natural sympathies in a strong emphasis on the side of the importance of the conceptions of the divine unchangeableness and impassibility."[10]

After a most detailed study, Lilla enumerates the main tenets of Clement's doctrine of God; we quote only the ones more pertinent to our study:

> God is incorporeal, formless, and
> without any attribute;
> he is very difficult to reach,
> far away from the sensible world,
> above space and time;
> he cannot be comprehended by the human mind:
> in other words, he is 'unknown';
> he is ineffable;
> the best way to approach him which
> the human mind possesses is
> the negative process.[11]

In many aspects of this doctrine of God, Clement is heavily dependent on Philo. "Clement lays a strong emphasis on the fact that God has no human shape and is also devoid of any human quality. In this idea he is closely dependent on Philo."[12] "The transcendence of God necessarily implies his aloofness. He is very difficult to reach, and always keeps himself far away from those who want to approach him. For this topic also Philo is Clement's direct source."[13] "Many a scholar has pointed out the great similarity between Clement's conceptions of the Logos and of the highest divinity and those of Philo."[14] Certain expressions describing God as the one who cannot be circumscribed were first used by Philo and it was from him that Clement acquired them.[15]

Why this emphasis on Clement's dependence on Philo? To show that Clement too accepted as scriptural notions what in reality were the result of philosophical influence. A century and a half before him, Philo had made the critical decisions by substituting "spirituality" for "otherness" in God, and coming up with attributes of God in keeping with the qualities of the Platonic ideas. By Clement's time, these assumptions are so commonplace that Clement simply uses them without bothering to delve any deeper into the scriptural witness. They become blocks in the structure of his comprehensive system.

Of the several points Lilla mentioned as comprising

Clement's doctrine of God, we shall expand briefly on only one or two which are more pertinent to our topic. One of the things I wish to show here is how Clement's God has the characteristics of *thought*, of the left hemisphere. In Clement, this way of knowing (and consequently of "clothing") God reaches a high point in Christian theology; from him it descends to Origen, the Gregories, and subsequently to the whole Eastern and Western traditions. The *biblical* God was known intuitively; consequently he is vibrant, powerful, dynamically related to men and history. The God of Clement is just the opposite:

> Thence says the apostle: 'Now we see as through a glass but then face to face,' by sole pure and uncorporeal applications of the intellect. In reasoning, it is possible to divine respecting God, if one attempt without any of the sense, by reason, to reach what is individual; and do not quit the sphere of existences, till, rising up to the things which transcend it, he apprehends by the intellect itself that which is good, moving in the very confines of the world of thought, according to Plato.
>
> *Stromata*, V,xi,

> Now the sacrifice which is acceptable to God is unswerving abstraction from the body and its passions. This is the really true piety. And is not, on this account, philosophy rightly called by Socrates the practice of Death? For he who neither employs his eyes in the exercise of thought, nor draws aught from his other senses, but with pure mind itself applies to objects, practises the true philosophy. This is, then, the import of the silence of five years prescribed by Pythagoras, which he enjoined on his disciples; that, in abstracting themselves from the objects of sense, they might with the mind alone contemplate the Deity. It was from Moses that the chief of the Greeks drew these philosophical tenets. For he commands holocausts to be skinned and divided into parts. For the gnostic soul must be consecrated to the light, stript of all the integuments of matter, devoid of the frivolousness of the body

and of all the passions, which are acquired through vain and lying opinions, and divested of the lusts of the flesh. But most men, clothed with what is perishable, like cockles, and rolled all round in a ball in their excesses, like hedgehogs, entertain the same ideas of the blessed and incorruptible God as of themselves. But it has escaped their notice that though they be near to us, that God has bestowed on us ten thousand things in which He does not share: birth, being Himself unborn; food, He wanting nothing; and growth, He always being equal; and long life and immortality, He being immortal and incapable of growing old. Wherefore let no one imagine that hands, and feet, and mouth, and eyes, and going in and coming out, and resentments and threats, are said by the Hebrews to be attributes of God. By no means; but that certain of these appellations are used more sacredly in an allegorical sense, which, as the discourse proceeds, we shall explain at the proper time.

Stromata, V,xi

This passage is very typical of Clement. Osborn says that it expresses a tenet of the Middle Platonism of the times whereby God can only be known by abstracting all qualities from our idea of a thing.[16] Clement says quite clearly that "familiarity with the sight disparages the reverence for what is divine" (V,v). "It is this kind of language which leads M. de Faye to say that Clement's God, metaphysically considered, is a mere negation, and that the influence of philosophy upon Clement was rationalistic."[17]

In our section on the Old Testament we put a good deal of emphasis on the Hebrew concept of the Name. What is Clement's approach to the names of God in the scriptures? "And therefore it[God] is without form or name. And if we name it we do not do so properly, terming it either the One, or the Good, or the Mind, or Absolute Being, or Father, or God, or Creator, or Lord. We speak not as supplying His name; but for want, we use good names, in order that the mind may have these as points of support, so as not to err in other respects" (V,xii).

"Clement is most definite on this point. Strictly speaking, we cannot talk about God."[18] "Clement is not concerned with degrees of truth, nor does he consider these names are nearer the limit of truth than other names. All names are incorrect. A name or names are necessary for disclosure. Ethical considerations determine that names should be good ones. But strictly speaking, the names are not names at all. God can have no name."[19]

Nevertheless, when speaking briefly about God's name in Ex 3:14, Clement is aware of the *future* dimension of the Hebrew of which we spoke in the first chapter. "Jave, which is interpreted 'Who is and shall be'" (V,ii). "Further, the mystic name of four letters which was affixed to those alone to whom the adytum was accessible, is called Jave, which is interpreted 'Who is and shall be'" (V,vi). But he draws no conclusions from this.

My comment on all this would be that Clement, by sheer reasoning power, ascends by abstraction to the conclusion that God cannot be spoken about: "For how can that be expressed which is neither genus, nor difference, nor species, nor individual, nor number, nay more, is neither an event, nor that to which an event happens" (V,xii)? Clement does not see the names of God in scripture conveying any knowledge worthy of note. "For predicates are expressed either from what belongs to things themselves, or from their mutual relation" (V,xii). For Clement, God cannot be in real relation: "We cannot speak of God as having a relation to anything else, because this would mean a loss of remoteness, and a distinction between the One and the One as related to that being."[20] Names have a pedagogical function and so we must have a care in choosing them. But *nomina sunt realia*, the function of names in the scriptures, would not be Clement's view at all.

In the passage we have been quoting, Clement offers a

reflection which is the contention of this book, although he probably does not mean it in the same way. He says: "Each one [name] by itself does not express God; but all together are indicative of the power of the Omnipotent" (V,xii). Precisely! *All* the names and predicates of God, in both scripture and philosophy—even Clement's Unknowable One—have a place, and express part of the truth about God. Since the reality, God, is complex, indeed the most complex, no single name or philosophical conclusion can express who he is. Clement's mistake, like Philo's, was to believe that the philosophical truth—that God is ultimately beyond all names—is a deeper truth than his name, Yahweh.

Clement's doctrine of God is of a piece with his concept of man, and one sheds light on the other. "For Clement, to be raised above passion is the ideal set before the Christian Gnostic, the deification of which corresponds to that permanent condition of God who is 'without passion, without anger, without desire. . . .' The mixture of Christian elements such as spring from a noble and austere ethical philosophy...lacks the true humanity of Christianity. Alongside of all the excellent instruction which he gives on the Christian's faithfulness and self-control, his purity, and, above all, his love of God...there runs the notion of passionlessness as in and for itself a supreme moral excellence. The advanced Christian will be out of the reach not only of the wrong sort of pleasurable emotions, but of all pleasurable emotions" (Stromata, VII,xi,14).[21]

In the preceding chapter we saw some of the meanings of *apatheia*. Clement will take the word one step beyond the school-Platonism of the second century. He does this when he considers *apatheia* as the highest ethical ideal, and when he identifies it with the "likeness to God."[22] "Wherefore also man is said 'to have been made in God's image and likeness.' For the image of God is the divine and royal Word, the impassible man; and the image of the image is the human mind" (Stromata, V,xiv).

Virtue, for Clement, is destroying the irrational *pathe*. "This is not the case of God who, being *apathes* by his own nature, has no need of virtue."[23]

Whatever the word meant in earlier times, Clement is quite explicit in what *he* means by it. "Passionlessness is the perfect fruit of the eradication of all desire." Thus, Jesus himself "was altogether impassible, into Him no movement of passion could find its way, neither pleasure nor pain." The Apostles also "were subject to no emotional change, so that even the emotions which seem good, courage, zeal, joy, desire could not be attributed to them. Nothing can affect the perfect man so as to evoke any of these emotions."[24] And man is the image of God. God, then, has no passions.

Clement is a man of great faith. In faith he knows that Jesus is the true Door to knowledge of the Father. In a passage which Danielou describes as "an epoch in the history of human thought,"[25] Clement concludes:

> It remains that we understand the Unknown by divine grace, and by the Word alone that proceeds from Him; as Luke in the Acts of the Apostles relates that Paul said: 'Men of Athens, I perceive that in all things you are very religious people. For in walking about, and looking at the objects of your worship, I found an altar on which was inscribed "To an Unknown God." Whom therefore you ignorantly worship, him I declare unto you.' *Stromata*, V,xii

The "men of Athens" are all those who seek to come to a knowledge of God through reason alone.

In many places, Clement affirms that Jesus is the only door to true knowledge of God: ". . .for by the Son is the Father known" (V,i); "the Son is the true Teacher in respect to the Father" (V,i). Osborn writes concerning this passage:

> The One, Unknown in himself, is understood by what proceeds from him, namely his Logos. In this passage we pass from philosophy to religion. God transcends logical categories

and all the names that might be given him. Other ways of knowledge being excluded, one possibility is left. It is that we perceive the unknown God by his grace and by the Logos that comes from him.26

And Danielou writes of this turning-point in Clement's thought:

> The place of Greek philosophy within the Christian system will now be clear. A certain knowledge of God, namely knowledge of him as manifested in his works, is innate in every man. Philosophy, by the process of abstraction, purifies this concept of God of its anthropomorphisms, and thus arrives at the negative theology, the quest of the invisible, the affirmation that no existent reality can be predicated of God. Farther than this, however, it cannot go. Only the Son who has within himself the knowledge of the Father, can introduce Man to this knowledge. The new thing in Christianity is essentially the revelation of the Son, both in the sense of the knowledge that there is a Son, and also of the fact that he alone can bring men to the knowledge of the unknowable.27

One would tend to think that since Clement has seen that only through Jesus can we arrive at a true knowledge of God, he would go on to develop the point. But he does not—at least, the authors never go into it, which makes me presume it is not central to his teaching on the knowledge of God. Clement's legacy to us as far as the knowledge of God is concerned centers around his method of abstraction and his "negative" theological terms.

One reason for his failure to develop this insight may be because his philosophy colored everything, even his notion of Jesus. If Jesus, too, is seen in Platonic terms, we will still receive from him the same kind of knowledge. Clement writes:

> "Now the Word of God says, 'I am the truth.' The Word is then to be contemplated by the mind. 'Do you aver,' it was said, 'that there are any true philosophers?' 'Yes,' said I, 'those

who love to contemplate the truth.' In the Phaedus, Plato, speaking of the truth, shows that it is an idea. Now an idea is a conception of God; and this the barbarians (Jews) have called the Word of God" (*Stromata*, V,iii). "If then we affirm that aught is just, and affirm it to be good, and we also say that truth is something, yet we have never seen any such objects with our eyes, but with our mind alone. Now the Word of God says, 'I am the truth.' The Word is then to be contemplated by the mind" (V,ii).

His theological principle was sound, namely, that only the Word can give true knowledge about God. Because of his Platonism, however, he could not arrive at a more human understanding of Jesus and the ways Jesus teaches us about the Father.

Another indication of the priority Clement gives to philosophical knowledge is this: it is so specialized that it is reserved for the few.

In the gospel, Jesus' invitation is open to all. If anyone loves him, his Father will come also, dwell with that person, and reveal who he is. In a real sense then, true knowledge of God through the Word is accessible to all. For Clement, however, "true knowledge of God" is reserved to a few: "For great is the crowd that keep to the things of sense, as if they were the only things in existence. But the knowledge of God is a thing inaccessible to the ears and like organs of this kind of people" (*Stromata*, V,iii). Lilla comments: "The contemplation of the highest divinity which can only be attained by means of an allegorical interpretation of Scripture, in which philosophy plays an important role, represents an object of esoteric knowledge, which can be communicated only to a few."[28]

I think this stance, that knowledge of God is really only accessible to a select few, is one of the greatest arguments *against* giving priority to philosophical knowledge of God. In one real sense, the deepest, the most necessary, and the most true knowledge about God must be accessible to *all* through the heart, intuition, and grace—that is, through relationship with Jesus. Not that this is the only kind of knowledge, or that philosophical knowledge has no place, but the great gift of knowing God cannot depend on how many books a person has read, or how fine a mind he has to understand abstract philosophical questions. The deepest knowledge about God comes through relationship with the Word. All other knowledge must be guided by this.

No doubt, Clement's doctrine of the knowledge of God is much more subtle and refined than I have presented it. What is indisputable is his role in fostering negative concepts about God, and helping to create the impression that these are somehow more perfect ways of speaking about God. But Clement was a pioneer in theology. It is not surprising that he was unsuccessful "in combining ideas of God which rest upon a basis of abstractions... with a theology which claims to find the religious and moral relationships in which God stands to men the surest clue to the understanding of the divine nature...."[29] That problem, after two centuries, has still not been solved!

Before leaving the city of Alexandria, a few words must be said about Origen. "A few words," not because he was a lesser light than Philo or Clement; he was not. However, from my studies, it seems that the crucial decisions concerning God's impassibility were made before Origen, and that he accepts this traditional position. When it is said that Origen's teaching on the impassibility of God "is in line with the teaching of Clement,"[30] it means that with Origen the main lines of this doctrine are finalized, and from this school they pass into the permanent bloodstream of the Church. It is because of this that our study can conclude with Origen.

Origen (185-254) lived most of his life in Alexandria and was steeped in the same traditions as was Clement. He was the first real systematic theologian and one of the greatest (if not the greatest) Christian thinkers of all times.

The impact of his work on all future theology is incalculable.

In one of his early and most influential works, *On First Principles*, Origen responds to the question of how feelings can be attributed to God in the Old Testament when God is impassible. Origen's reply, in good Alexandrian fashion, is that we must look for the *spiritual meaning*. And, in his great work *Against Celsus*, Origen teaches that the sayings of the Old Testament were spoken "as though God were subject to human affections. We do not therefore ascribe human passions to God, nor do we hold impious opinions about Him."[31] In a few words, Bigg gives us Origen's doctrine of God: "Being incorporeal, God is independent of the laws of Space and Time, omniscient, omnipresent, unchanging, incomprehensible."[32] "God being unchanging, eternal, must needs be passionless."[33] Such would be Origen's main positions on the question with which we are concerned.

However, as Origen neared the end of his life (in Caesarea), he was more and more crushed by misunderstanding, and perhaps, too, by a premonition of his own impending physical torture for Christ's sake. We have many of the homilies he preached during this period. In several, there are insights into the pathos of God which, unfortunately, neither he nor his successors developed. They would offer fruitful material for anyone seeking to work out a doctrine of pathos from Christian tradition.

In his homily on the Sixteenth chapter of Ezechiel, Origen said:

> He descended to earth in pity for the human race. He suffered our sufferings before He suffered the Cross and thought it right to take upon Him our flesh. For if He had not suffered, He would not have come to take part in human life. First did He suffer, then He descended and was seen. What is that passion which He suffered for us? Love is passion. The Father also Himself, and the God of all things, longsuffering and very pitiful and compassionate, does He not in some way suffer?

> Can you be ignorant of this, that when He deals with human things He suffers a human passion? 'For the Lord thy God endured thy ways as if a man should endure his son.' Therefore God endures our ways inasmuch as the Son of God bears our sufferings. The Father Himself is not impassible. If He is besought, He is pitiful and compassionate, He suffers something of love, and in those things in which because of the greatness of His nature He cannot subsist, He shares, and because of us He endures human sufferings.[34]

(As the reader will recall, Ezechiel 16 is the incredibly beautiful allegory of Israel, the unfaithful wife, of how Yahweh picked her up from the gutter, washed her and clothed her as his bride.)

The second reference is in his homily on the Book of Numbers, the twenty-eighth chapter. He is speaking about the meaning of feast days, and he says:

> ...wonderful perhaps it is what I wish to say; we give to God and the angels reasons for festivity and joy; we who are on earth give heaven its occasion for joy and exaltation....But as our good actions and our progress in virtue give birth to joy and festivity for God and the angels, so I fear lest our evil conversation be the cause of lamentations and sorrows not on earth only but in heaven as well, and lest the sins of men stir up sorrow perchance even for God Himself. It is certain that where joy is felt for that which is good, there for that which is contrary thereunto lamentation follows: if therefore they rejoice over him who is converted, of necessity they must grieve for the sinner.[35]

However, he seems to feel that he has been carried too far by his religious sensibilities, and adds:

> Now all these sayings in which God is spoken of as sorrowing or rejoicing or hating or being glad are to be understood as uttered by Scripture after an allegorical and human manner. The divine nature is altogether separated from every affection of passion and change, and remains unmoved and unshaken forever on that peak of blessedness.[36]

These two thoughts, so close together in the mind of Origen that day as he preached, are a fitting representation of the dilemma posed by the scriptural witness. On the one hand were the real emotions ascribed to God and the real sufferings of Jesus the God-Man; on the other hand was the conclusion of philosophy that God cannot change. Because of the "horizon" of the times, it probably was not possible for any one in the second century to entertain for very long the notion of the passibility of God: "To assert the reality of 'passion' in God in such a way as not to expose His nature to a process of change which must imply a measure of deterioration was beyond their power."[37]

"The Father Himself is not impassible," said Origen, "He has the passion of love." "God is love," said St. John. This religious intuition that God is love was not taken into consideration in the first two centuries when the groundwork for the transcendence of God was being laid. Part of a theology of pathos will depend on just such a development. But here we end our intellectual investigation.

9. The Passionate

S. D. Goitein...has suggested that the tetragrammaton is related to the Hebrew root hwy (and the Arabic hawa), the basic meaning of which is passionate love and devotion to some aim. 'The name has the usual form of the imperfect—as, e.g. the names of Isaac and Jacob—and means therefore, "He who acts passionately, the Passionate." '

> Abraham Heschel, *The Prophets*

If man is presented with the so-called revelation of his radical inutility, how is he going to avoid distaste for action?...In point of fact, what gives life to Christianity is not the sense of the created world's contingency, but the sense of the mutual completion of God and the world.

> Teilhard de Chardin, *Christianisme et evolution*
> quoted by Christopher Mooney in
> *Teilhard de Chardin and the Mystery of Christ*

'Open both your ears. If a man suffers
   all alone, it is clear, his suffering remains
   within him, right?'
'Right,' Ernie said.
'But if another looks at him and says to him:
   "How you suffer, brother Jew...," what
   happens then?'
'I understand that too. He takes the suffering
   of his friend into his eyes.'
'And if he is blind, do you think he can do
   that?'
'Of course, through his ears!'

'And if he is deaf?'
'Then through his hands.'
'And if the other is far away, if he can neither
   hear him nor see him, and not even touch him,
   do you believe then that he can take in his pain?'
'Maybe he can sense it.'
'You've said it, my love, that is exactly
   what the Just Man does! He senses all the
   evil on the earth, and he takes it into his
   heart!'
'But what good does it do to sense it, if
   nothing is changed?'
'It changes for God, don't you see?'

Andre Schwarz-Bart, *The Last of the Just*

Man is challenged to participate in the suffering of God at the hands of a Godless world.

Dietrich Bonhoeffer, *Prisoner for God*

I believe that the foregoing study has shown the unsuccessful attempt of Greek philosophical concepts to clarify the biblical intuitions of God's pathos. "Nowhere is this bad influence of Greek philosophical presuppositions on Christian thinking about God more clearly to be seen than in what are commonly known as the traditional attributes of God, and in particular the attribute of impassibility."[1] The unrelated, unpathetic, unaffected God is not the God of the scriptures, but of philosophy. Philosophy can also be a word of God, but its truth must be judged by the scriptural and faith intuitions, not the other way around. In this final chapter I wish to recapitulate and tie together some loose ends; also, to suggest some approaches to a doctrine of God's pathos.

One of the components of this doctrine would be a fuller treatment of God's characteristics as known through the biblical revelation. Such studies already exist, and they would simply need to be related more specifically to our topic.

The studies on the left and right hemispheres of the brain, and on Greek and Hebrew thought-patterns, were meant as aids to an appreciation of this priority of the scriptural witness. By showing the assets and liabilities of each mode of thought, I hoped to show that if reason and intuition do not work together as complementary, truth becomes distorted. I believe I have shown how the intuition of God's pathos became distorted by an overemphasis on the rational as opposed to the intuitive.

What has not formed a part of this study, but which must eventually find a place in any approach to the problem, is some kind of form-criticism of the Church's teaching on this point. All doctrinal statements on God's immutability are *subsequent* to the period examined in this book. There are still many questions of a dogmatic nature involved in dealing with such statements in the light of my historical critique. Having said that, perhaps a few words in relation to this aspect would be in order.

I would like to return for a moment to some of J. C. Murray's remarks, specifically about the meaning of the Council of Nicea for the theological enterprise. I think they are very significant for the present question.

Murray said that the word finally chosen to settle the question of the Son's relation to the Father—*homousion* (same substance)—meant essentially several very important things for theology itself. First, it was a rejection of the view that the formulation of the Christian faith must be restricted to biblical phrases. Secondly, it established the stature of the ontological mentality within the Church. Thirdly, the two later Councils (Ephesus and Chalcedon) by expanding on Nicea, indicated that the Church forbids the freezing of the Christian faith in patristic formulas. Fourthly, by sanctioning the passage from scriptural to ontological categories, Nicea sanctioned the principle of the development of doctrine—"one might better speak of growth in understanding of the primitive affirmations contained in the New Testament revelation." And finally, Nicea established the stature of the philosophical reason in the field of theology.[2]

The basic contentions and conclusions of this present study fit in very well, I think, with Murray's observations; his points would also serve as good guidelines for an approach to the dogmatic questions. The present study does not say that only biblical categories are proper when speaking about God. Nor does it advocate a return to such categories, pure and simple. I believe in the validity of an ontological approach to try and express what God-is-in-himself. I believe also that it is legitimate to try and expand on patristic formulas, as Murray says, and that *therefore it is legitimate for us now to try and expand on the formulas of early Councils regarding the immutability of God.*

I believe that the goal in this matter of God's pathos is to grow in an understanding of the affirmations of the faith as contained in the New Testament, denying that the ontological notion of impassibility does this adequately.

Thus, the question arises: is the ontological notion of the impassibility of God, so often used by the Fathers, a "final word" as *homousion* was a final word? That is to say, was the question of impassibility ever made the subject of real debate and discussion at a Council so that this teaching is not merely uncritical and unreflective, but critical and consciously adopted?

In one sense, there was a certain finality to the word *homousion*. Not that future generations cannot come up with other metaphysical categories to express the Son's relation to the Father, but they will have to say *the same thing as homousion*, namely, that the Son is of the same substance as the Father. It is final as to its meaning for the faith, but not final in its expression.

Can the same kind of finality be claimed for impassibility? It means, as we have seen, that God does not change at all. Without doubt, this is what the Fathers of early Councils meant by it. But was the word consciously and deliberately chosen, so that we could say that the Fathers of the Church in Council were satisfied that this word rightly expressed the biblical affirmation of God's constancy, faithfulness, his "not being like a man," or whatever scriptural attitude of God we wish to align with impassibility? What is the status, in tradition, of impassibility? Is the sense in which the Fathers understood it final, as the sense of *homousion* is final? That is a question that needs to be examined.

It seems to me that our scriptural and religious intuitions have no problem with God being affected by what we do. The crisis is in the realm of abstract, theological and philosophical thinking about the problem. Many of our basic thoughts about God, man and the world are a fusion of philosophy and the scriptural witness. Scripture scholars are telling us just how little about the world can be "proved" from scripture. Scripture contains religious intuitions about reality. These are very simple, uncritical, open-ended statements. The full fleshing-out of such statements, which then becomes part of our doctrinal understanding, is a fusion of scripture with thought from other areas of human knowledge. This fusion is an ongoing process, and in the process the teachings are modified and clarified. The question raised by this book is whether or not the doctrine of God's immutability is one of the teachings which ought to be modified in the light of new knowledge about man and his world—and our present understanding of the scriptures. My answer would be yes.

Avery Dulles, in his book *Models of the Church*, utilizes a model approach to the Church which could be used in regard to the mystery of God himself; the pathos of God would be one of these models.

Dulles quotes Pope Paul as saying that "the Church is a mystery. It lies, therefore, within the very nature of the Church to be always open to new and ever greater exploration."[3] If this is true of the mystery of the Church, how much more is it true of the mystery of God himself! "If man's knowledge of God is to be real it must grow in an unending cyclic process...man must continually press on toward knowledge and experience in the indeterminate future and not rest with the notion of a God caught somehow in the net of concepts at a moment in his past."[4]

Dulles notes that Gustave Weigel pointed out a theological shift at the Council. It was a shift away from Aristotelian definitions to biblical images. The bible, Dulles says, is replete with images, and these images are one type of model. An image is a word or a phrase which when employed reflectively and critically, helps to deepen our understanding of a reality.[5] An image is a model that can be imagined. In regard to the Church, "Sheepfold" would be an image and "Society" would be a model.

Besides the bible as a source of images, the religious experience of people is also an important element in the development of symbols. Dulles quotes John Powell to the effect that there is a discernment and a connaturality among the faithful which can serve as a guide to models.[6] The thesis of Dulles' book on the Church is that a legitimate theology of the Church would incorporate the values of all legitimate models.

The application of this approach to our present question is obvious. The images we have of God in the bible, including his pathos, would be a collection of models to be taken into consideration when seeking an understanding of God's nature. By way of example, each of the chapter headings of this book could be taken as an image or model. God's reality, as far as human words can attain, should be described by all these models together, each one emphasizing a different aspect of God.

Some readers who have persevered this far in the book may be quite nervous by now. It may seem to them that by questioning the impassibility of God I am trying to tear the veil from the mystery of God. I believe I am attempting just the opposite. *I believe that to over-*

emphasize only one model (in this case, the philosophical model of impassibility), is to remove the mystery from God. We leave God's nature much more to mystery if we allow the passible/impassible paradox to remain.

The pathos of God as described in this book seems to me to meet Dulles' criterion for a valid model: "A model is accepted if it accounts for a large number of biblical and traditional data and accords with what history and experience tell us about the Christian life."[7] Meaningful models have "the capacity to lead to new theological insights."[8] "Thanks to the ongoing experience of the Christian community, theology can discover aspects of the gospel of which Christians were not previously conscious."[9]

I mentioned my belief earlier that the impassibility of God is a paradigm in the general thinking of the Church. Dulles writes: "As a model succeeds in dealing with a number of different problems, it becomes an object of confidence, sometimes to such an extent that theologians almost cease to question its appropriateness for almost any problem that may arise."[10] This attitude is certainly attached to the doctrine of God's impassibility. It is reflected in Donceel's imaginary interlocutor who, as soon as the question of mutability in God is broached, ends the conversation abruptly. It is one of those "unthinkable thoughts" that few serious-minded people allow themselves to dwell upon for too long. It is a paradigm.

But Dulles says (and I think his insight has a great deal to do with the resistance to the pathos of God) that "theologians who ought to be able to shift their thinking from one key to another, often resist new paradigms because these eliminate problems on which they have built up a considerable expertise, and introduce other problems with regard to which they have no special competence."[11] The thesis of this book is that the pathos of God ought to be considered as one of the models (images) for speaking about the mystery of God. Instead of exalting one model or image over another—impassibility over possibility—it would be more accurate to recognize that the manifold images given us by scripture and tradition are mutually complementary. They should be made to interpenetrate and mutually qualify one another.[12]

This notion of paradigm suggests another avenue for future exploration in relation to the religious experience of the Christian people.

Each community, whether ecclesial, cultural, scientific or whatever, operates according to paradigms. These have been defined as "shared conceptions of what is possible, the boundaries of acceptable inquiry, the limiting cases."[13] Basically they are fixed mentalities or concepts, often unquestioned or unexamined, of the limits of reality. A little story quoted by Ornstein brings out the meaning very well:

> A man, having looted a city, was trying to sell an exquisite rug, one of the spoils. 'Who will give me 100 pieces of gold for this rug?' he cried throughout the town. After the sale was completed, a comrade approached the seller and asked, 'Why did you not ask more for that priceless rug?' 'Is there any number higher than 100?' asked the seller.

Evidently the seller had come from a land where counting was in an early stage of development! He could not possibly have asked for more because he didn't know more could be asked for. The number 100 was a paradigm for him, a mind-set which put limits on his approach to reality, in this case, selling.

In one sense, all dogmas are mind-sets, paradigms. Not every individual has examined and worked through each tenet of the faith, nor is it necessary or possible to do so. The Church, down through the ages, has prayed over and lived out these mysteries in her life with her Spouse, and then articulated her faith in certain words. All this is part of her role and our heritage. It is proper, then, that these teachings structure our own religious psyches; God's impassibility is one of these paradigms.

But I believe that a study of the saints and mystics of the Church would also reveal the model/image of God's *pathos*. To cite one of countless examples. One of the most frequently quoted sayings of the Little Flower is this: "How the good God *thirsts* for the love of his creatures." Dulles said that the experience of Christians is also a criterion for discovering models of the mysteries of faith. I believe that notwithstanding the Church's doctrine of God's immutability, the pathos of God frequently comes through the religious consciousness of God's people in their life with him. I believe this corporate and universal experience confirms the pathos of God as a model, a legitimate model to be used in our theology of God.

I have said several times, and in a variety of ways in this book, that the problem of speaking of God's pathos lies more in the realm of philosophy than any place else; indeed, it was philosophical concepts which were given precedence over the biblical. In this final chapter I would like to introduce the reader to a philosophical trend today which I think could help clarify some of our thinking about the pathos of God, and which has had a great deal to do with my own rethinking of this problem. This trend is the school of philosophers and theologians who are using the metaphysics of A. N. Whitehead as an intellectual tool to grapple with the nature of reality.

I shall not presume here to try and present Whitehead's doctrine of God. The bibliography contains references for anyone who wishes to pursue it. What I have in mind is much more general, and simple. I wish to introduce readers (if introduction is necessary) to Whitehead's name and give some feel for his importance today in the philosophical and theological worlds. Then, I wish to indicate how some of the process thinkers are criticizing the traditional doctrine of God, especially in those areas relative to God's pathos. Finally, returning to the thought of Abraham Heschel with which this book began, I wish to show how process thought and biblical intuition can complement each other in this matter of God's pathos.

For those who are unaware of it, there is a new trend in philosophical theology today. It is a school of thinkers, mostly in America but broadening out into ever-widening circles, using the metaphysics of A. N. Whitehead as a conceptuality to interpret the themes of the Christian faith.[14] They represent a specific branch of the whole movement of process thought, of which the Teilhardian school is another dimension. Actually, the whole mentality of modern man consists in a processive, evolutionary view of reality; such a mind-set forms an essential part of modern man's horizon.

Whitehead's fundamental notion is that reality at its core is in process of becoming. The heart of every reality is an happening, an occurrence, an event or, in his own technical language, an "actual occasion." The Scholastics used to say, *natura non fit per saltum*, "nature does not operate according to leaps." Whitehead's philosophy would say exactly the opposite: *"natura fit per saltum."* At the core of reality is motion, events, leaps, sudden explosions of energy. In his major work, *Process and Reality*, Whitehead spells out the implications of this doctrine.

And how does he arrive at this conclusion? By several paths. He says that the only reality we truly know is our own internal experience. If all of reality is not somehow of a piece with this experience, then we cannot know it at all. Also, modern atomic physics attests to the fact that all things are in motion, in process, in a state of becoming.

In some way, change is found even in God. We know of nothing in the whole universe that is static and unchanging. Whatever is actual is finite. God cannot change in what is essential to him as God, but he can change in non-essential matters, in his "consequent nature," as Whitehead would say, that is, in that part of God which is turned toward the world.

Perhaps it is more harmful than helpful to mention only this much about Whitehead's doctrine of God, leaving room for all sorts of misunderstandings and questions and problems. But it has to be risked. Again, I refer the interested reader to the relevant material (especially Cobb's books) which will do much to assuage fears and questions.

In the opinion of many, the Whiteheadian school is one fruitful philosophical tool for theology today. David Tracy, professor of philosophy at the University of Chicago, has recently characterized this particular trend:

> My fundamental hope is that other members of the American Catholic community [might] recognize that the process thinkers have articulated a challenge to our usual way of thinking which no serious participant in our present moment can long ignore. These thinkers merit the authentic gratitude of us all for forcing reflection upon the one fundamental theological question—the question of God.[15]

Whitehead first presented his doctrine of God in his book *Science and the Modern World*. The bulk of this book comprises the Lowell Lectures for 1925, although the chapters on "Abstraction" and "God" were not part of the original lectures. For all his intellectual power, Whitehead was well aware that rational, logical thinking was not the only avenue to reality. In his next book, *Religion In the Making*, "Whitehead proposed that religion contributes its own independent evidence which metaphysics must take into account in framing its description. . . ." In his previous thinking Whitehead had put more emphasis on the dependence of religious knowledge on the philosophical. In *Religion* he emphasizes their reciprocity.[16]

Whitehead states quite plainly that metaphysical knowledge about God is not the whole story:

> What further can be known about God must be sought in the region of particular experiences, and therefore rests on an empirical basis. In respect to the interpretation of these experiences, mankind has differed profoundly. He has been named respectively Jehovah, Allah, Brahma, Father in Heaven, Order of Heaven, First Cause, Supreme Being, Chance.[17]

Whitehead, realist that he was, knew that reality was not abstract. It is a swirling, blinding explosion of life and movement. He knew well that the rational mind had the power to reduce reality to an abstraction: "Thought is abstract; the intolerant use of abstractions is the major vice of the intellect."[18]

Whitehead's doctrine of God was very sketchy and undeveloped. Much work has and is being done to develop this aspect of his thought. Charles Hartshorne is considered by many to be the greatest, living exponent of Whitehead's thought, particularly on the question of God. The problem as Hartshorne and many others see it is that in the history of philosophical theology certain notions of a more metaphysical nature became the ultimate criteria, and the intuitive, religious insights of man about God were subordinated to philosophy. In his 1963 preface to an earlier work, *The Divine Relativity*, Hartshorne wrote, "I am convinced that 'classical theism' (as much Greek as Christian, Jewish, or Islamic) was an incorrect translation of the central religious idea into philosophical categories."[19] The "central religious idea" is God.

More specifically, what are these process thinkers saying about the history of the doctrine of God? They are saying that the two trends in natural theology—the trend which emphasizes God as "self-sufficient," and the trend which emphasizes him as "outgoing"—have never been successfully reconciled.[20] They think that there has been "a persistent tendency, not least among theologians...to deprecate the empirical element in religion, and to exalt God beyond the reach of human contact. If He is so represented, it will be impossible to get Him back again. If we start from the assumptions of ordinary religion, we shall be able to include in a subordinate role the insights of philosophers."[21] These thinkers exegete the history of philosophical theology in the most exact way and show that there are alternatives to the conception of God as the "Completely Unaffected One," alternatives which have not been given due consideration.

The book which has best done this task to date is *Philosophers Speak About God* by Hartshorne and William Reese. Schubert Ogden has called this book something like a Heideggerian "dismantling" (Destruktion) of the history of philosophical theology. In the Introduction to this book, Hartshorne gives a brief overview of what, in his estimation, happened. What follows is the briefest of summaries of his main criticism.

Man's intellect, Hartshorne says, tends to oversimplification. The idea of God first arose in an emotional, practical form, in the Old Testament and in the Upanishads. If nothing was sharply defined in these early periods, neither was anything sharply excluded. The first attempts to define, analyse and purify in Aristotle and Philo were one-sided. In Hartshorne's view, something of the following happened.

There were contrasting terms in philosophical systems such as being and becoming, one and many, permanency and change. Now these terms are mutually exclusive, that is to say, the realities they designate are mutually exclusive. A choice had to be made. Thinkers decided which of the pair was good, and then they proceeded to attribute the "good" characteristic to God in a supreme fashion. The other term of the contrast was wholly denied as "unworthy" of God. "Classical theism," Hartshorne says, "is the chief product of this method." Another name he uses is "monopolarity," or the selection of only "one pole" of the contrast.

Hartshorne simply says that choosing between, say, change and permanence, or between one and many, is not the only choice possible. He says there is good unity and bad unity, good passivity and bad passivity. Thus there can be good change and bad change. What we need to affirm, says Hartshorne, is *both poles* of a contrast in their best characteristics. He calls this the doctrine of "dipolarity," the incorporation of "both poles." Thus, this doctrine asserts that in God there is a good kind of passibleness and a good kind of impassibleness; also, there would be a bad kind of both that would be unworthy of God.

Hartshorne says that "classical theism and pantheism choose one side of the contrasts. Theism admits of plurality, potentiality, and becoming 'outside' of God, while pantheism supposes that God includes everything in himself, and therefore things like change and becoming are merely illusion."[22]

Such is a very brief statement of Hartshorne's doctrine of "panentheism" or dipolar theism. ("Neoclassical" is another name given to this doctrine.) He has spent a great deal of his life trying to flesh out the philosophical nuances of this doctrine. It is an effort which certainly merits the profound consideration of all Christian theologians.

What was my surprise then one day when I came across Abraham Heschel's book *The Prophets*! Here, from a deeply biblical viewpoint, Heschel had arrived at a conclusion similar to these process philosophers: there is a real pathos, an affectedness in God. Now, at the close of this book, I wish to return to Heschel's thought and use his words to speak about the reality of God's pathos.

In Jewish thought, according to Heschel, there is a uniqueness about the prophets' knowledge of God. "It is an act of boldness allowed only to the prophets to measure the Creator by the standard of the creature."[23] In a variety of ways, Heschel says that the prophets spoke as no men either before or after them have spoken. (Whitehead also occasionally cites the prophetic consciousness as a milestone in the history of mankind's religious life: "Our civilization owes to them [the prophets] more than we can express. They constitute one of the few groups of men who decisively altered history in any intimate sense." It is legitimate to say, I think, that this should also apply to their understanding of God's relationship to the world, which Heschel shall now describe for us.) I would like to quote directly from Heschel to show the beauty and the consistency of his thought:

> To the prophet...God does not reveal himself in an abstract absoluteness, but in a personal and intimate relation to the world. He is moved and affected by what happens in the world, and reacts accordingly. This notion that God can be intimately affected, that He possesses not merely intelligence and will, but also pathos, basically defines the prophetic consciousness of God.
> Pathos denotes, not an idea of goodness, but a living care...a dynamic relation between God and the world.
> God is concerned about the world and shares in its fate. Indeed, this is the essence of God's moral nature: His willingness to be intimately involved in the history of man.[24]

The second half of *The Prophets* is one of the most complete contemporary treatments of the philosophy, theology, etc. of pathos; it is highly recommended.

What a revolutionary book this was for me! Here was a renowned and highly respected Jewish theologian propounding a thesis on the pathos of God which fit in perfectly with what the process theologians were saying from their own perspective. This man, Heschel, who would not even pronounce the phrase "death of God" (as too blasphemous), did not consider the reality of the pathos of God as at all unworthy of God. On the contrary, he saw it as the deepest and as the most beautiful intuition of the prophets concerning God's relationship to us. It is still a great mystery to me why such a teaching has not brought forth appropriate comment and evaluation by our own Catholic theologians.

Catholic theologians are not the only ones to neglect the pathos of God. At the beginning of his recent book *God Suffers For Us*, Jung Lee has this to say:

> The concept of divine suffering...has been...almost completely ignored in important theological works of our time. Paul Tillich...in the last volume of his *Systematic Theology* states that present-day theology tries to avoid the issue of divine passibility, 'either by ignoring it or by calling it an inscrutable divine mystery. But such escape...is impossible in view of the question's significance for the most existential problem of theodicy....If theology refuses to answer such existential questions, it has neglected its task.' In spite of these remarks, he [Tillich] proceeds to give it only two pages out of nearly 1,000.[25]

A similar charge could be leveled at Catholic theologians. Scattered and fragmentary treatments can be found in scholarly tomes and in learned theological journals. Some of these have been used in this book; no doubt there are others. Still, I do not think there exists in English one book by a contemporary Catholic theologian which treats specifically or in any comprehensive fashion of the pathos or the affectedness of God. I do not know why. One of the purposes of this book is to stimulate more of a discussion on this matter.

Traditional theology has always taken Jesus as the starting point of its doctrines. Faith means that we take Jesus' view of reality before any other. All the great theologians understood this. To quote Danielou again, "Only the Word of God...can bring it [the human mind] to the knowledge of God as he is in himself." This is the theory. The contention of this book is that, in regard to the pathos of God, the Incarnation has not been as normative as it should have been.

> It might also be said that traditional theism is too much concerned about what God is in himself or his ontological attributes, and not enough about the moral attributes or what

God is for us. The 'in itself' in traditional theism has always been much more emphasized than the 'for us.' This is the basic problem raised by the Neoclassical Metaphysics and other tendencies stressing the immanence of God. To see in an ontological way the 'in-itself' of God and the 'for us' is still an unsolved problem. In this very difficult problem, philosophy will have to let itself be enlightened by the mystery of the Incarnation.[26]

Moltmann, whose work we have referred to earlier, has laid some groundwork for a theology of God's pathos stemming from the Incarnation.

He is very familiar with Heschel's work, and sees him as the first in modern times to "describe the prophets' proclamation of God as *pathetic* theology."[27] He admires Heschel's theology and then attempts to take it one step further as a Christian and make the Cross of Jesus the paradigm for a revelation of God's inner life.

We have already pointed out the strain in rabbinical tradition which saw a number of stages in the self-humiliation of God. Moltmann also points this out. There was, according to the rabbis, a self-humiliation of God in the creation, in the call of Abraham, Isaac and Jacob, in the exodus and in the exile. Christians would carry this one final step and say that the final self-humiliation of God was in the Cross of Jesus: "He emptied himself, taking the form of a servant, being born in the likeness of men. And being found in human form he humbled himself and became obedient unto death, even death on a cross" (Phil. 2:7-8).

The following passage is rather long but I trust that the reader enjoys literary citations as much as I do. It is a particularly beautiful passage, which sums up the religious motivation which prompted me to write this book. I quote from Father Gerald Vann's book:

> You may remember a scene towards the end of Helen Waddell's *Peter Abelard* in which Peter and Thibault hear a

terrible cry in the woods like the scream of a child in agony and they find a rabbit caught in a trap; they free it, and it nuzzles into Peter's arms and dies. 'It was that last confiding thrust that broke Abelard's heart. . . ."Thibault," he said, "do you think there is a God at all? Whatever has come to me, I earned it. But what did this one do?" Thibault nodded. "I know," he said. "only—I think God is in it too." Abelard looked up sharply. "In it? Do you mean that it makes Him suffer the way it does us?" Again Thibault nodded. . . ."All this," he stroked the limp body, "is because of us. But all the time God suffers. More than we do." Abelard looked at him, perplexed. . . . "Thibault, do you mean Calvary?" Thibault shook his head. "That was only a piece of it—the piece that we saw—in time. Like that." He pointed to a fallen tree beside them, sawn through the middle. "That dark ring there, it goes up and down the whole length of the tree. But you only see it where it is cut across. That is what Christ's life was; a bit of God that we saw. And we think God is like that, because Christ was like that, kind, and forgiving sins, and healing people. We think God is like that for ever, because it happened once, in Christ. But not the pain. Not the agony at the last. We think that stopped." Abelard looked at him. . . ."Then Thibault," he said slowly, "you think that all this. . .all this pain of the world, was Christ's cross?" "God's cross," said Thibault. "And it goes on." "The Patripassian heresy," muttered Abelard mechanically. "But, oh God, if it were true. Thibault, it must be true. At least, there is something at the back of it that is true. And if we could find it—it would bring back the whole world." '[28]

Yes, I believe there is something "at the back of it," something in our doctrine of God that has been left undeveloped and distorted. I do not know if the doctrine of God's pathos will bring back the whole world. Jesus hung on a tree for us, and if that does not draw men to love him, I cannot imagine what will.

But I do believe with Lee that "a meaningful question for suffering humanity in our times may have to do with our honest attempt to relate the concept of divine passibility to our existential situation."²⁹ Yes, I certainly believe *that* is true. I do not think an unrelated notion of God is the major stumbling block to belief. But I believe that the truth of God's pathos can immeasurably increase the love and devotion of believers, and make their life with God more exciting and alive. For the final meaning of all our sufferings and joys may be that they affect God as well, and that by this mutual relationship and interaction, both our lives receive everlasting enrichment.

The old rabbis of the early centuries were very wise and holy men; let us look at their solution to the anthropomorphic problem.

The rabbis were faced with the onslaught of Hellenism, the danger of transforming their living God into abstractions or some kind of impersonal "virtues of the soul." As we consider their response, let us keep in mind all the isms of our own day which try and tell us that man can no longer think of God as he used to, that we have out-grown childish notions, that we can no longer talk to a "Super-Person," and all the other sophisticated objections. Let us consider the solution of the rabbis before we cease speaking of God altogether! Nor need "intellectuals" get nervous. One of the curious features of the early centuries of our era was that the rabbis who were better acquainted —more learned, better educated—with Greek philosophy *were opposed* to allegory; it was the less informed who could not wait to turn the whole of scripture into images of Greek ideas.

The school which prevailed in Palestine was led by the great R. Akiba. He and his followers feared that "in divesting the heroes of the Bible of their real existence... the most vital forces of historic consciousness [would] become weakened and falsified."[30] To preserve the traditions of the past against all the persecutions and trials of the centuries requires something more than a God who is an allegory.[31] "What did it matter if pagans spread rumors that Jews in Jerusalem were ass-worshippers, or philosophers reproached Jews that their idea of God was not spiritual enough...? They sought the nearness of their God, craved for the presence of their Creator...."[32]

A vital, meaningful relationship with God, one that is more than an abstraction or a cultural appendage, cannot exist without using human terms when speaking about or to him. And when we say that God rejoices with us, gets angry because of our selfishness, is sad because of rejection by his people, what does it really mean? Is it poetry? Is it allegory for some deeper truth? If so, for what? Dear reader, what do *you* think such language means?

Marmorstein informs us that there was a rabbi who lived in Caesarea not too long after Origen, and his name was Abbahu. One day he preached a sermon in which he said: "Whenever salvation is granted to the Jews, this means simultaneously the salvation of the Holy One, blessed be He! Lord of the universe, Thou hast said 'with him I am in distress.' Be saved! By harkening to my supplication for redemption, come to Thine own salvation." "He (Abbahu) proclaimed that this idea of Israel's salvation being simultaneously the salvation of God, is taught in many passages of the Scriptures."[33]

The religious imagination is tempted here: Origen and this trend of thought in Caesarea at the same time. One relishes the picture of Origen as an old man having long, nightly conversations with the rabbis. We have seen that the theme of God's pathos appears in Origen's sermons from this period. After his long life of scholarship and metaphysical speculations, after years of meditation and prayer, is it possible that at the end of his life Origen learned from these rabbis one of the deepest of all mysteries, the pathos of God? "Lord of the Universe, Thou hast said, 'with him I am in distress,'" preached R. Abbahu. "The Father is not impassible," said Origen, "he suffers something of love."

APPENDIX A

It was thought that a listing of the characteristics of the left and right hemispheres would be helpful to the reader. The present table was drawn up by Joseph Bogen. It will show at a glance, and very clearly, findings regarding the two modes of thought which were arrived at by researchers working independently of each other. All the items in one column have something similar about them: the terms in the middle column express various aspects of the rational; all the terms in the third column express some aspect of intuition.

Who Proposed it?

Many Sources	Day	Night
Blackburn	Intellectual	Sensuous
Oppenheimer	Time, History	Eternity, Timelessness
Deikman	Active	Receptive
Polanyi	Explicit	Tacit
Levy, Speery	Analytic	Gestalt
Many Sources	Left Hemisphere	Right Hemisphere
Domhoff	Right (side)	Left (side)
Bogan	Proposition	Appositional
Lee	Lineal	Nonlineal
Luria	Sequential	Simultaneous
Semmes	Focal	Diffuse
Many Sources	Intellectual	Intuitive
Many Sources	Verbal	Spatial
Bacon	Argument	Experience*

*"The Other Side of the Brain: An Appositional Mind," in Ornstein, *Nature*, p. 111.

FOOTNOTES

Chapter 1

[1] (New York: Harper & Row Publishers, 1971), Vol. II, Chapter 1, "The Theology of Pathos."

[2] Juan Arias, *The God I Don't Believe In* (St. Meinrad's, Indiana: Abbey Press, 1973), p. 198.

[3] William J. Hill, O.P. "The Immutability of God," in *New Catholic Encyclopedia*, Vol. 7 (Catholic University of America, 1967), pp. 393-395.

[4] Henry Denzinger, *The Sources of Catholic Dogma*, trans. Roy J. Deferrari (St. Louis, Mo.: B. Herder Book Co., 1955).

[5] (Oxford: Blackfriars Publications, 1947), pp. 59-60.

[6] *Ibid.*, pp. 71, 75.

[7] "Second Thoughts On the Nature of God," *Thought*, Vol. XLVI, No. 182 (Autumn, 1971), pp. 348-349.

[8] *Ibid.*, pp. 355, 366.

[9] *Ibid.*, p. 355.

[10] *Ibid.*, p. 359.

[11] In *God Knowable and Unknowable* (New York: Fordham University Press, 1974), p. 43.

[12] *Ibid.*, p. 45.

[13] "Whitehead's Challenge To Theistic Realism," *New Scholasticism*, Vol. XXXVIII (January, 1964), p. 1.

[14] "Is God Really Related To the World?" *The American Catholic Philosophical Association Proceedings*, 1965, p. 145.

[15] *Ibid.*, p. 149.

[16] *The Early Christian Doctrine of God* (Charlottesville: University Press of Virginia, 1966), p. 64.

[17] *Teilhard de Chardin and the Mystery of Christ* (New York: Harper and Row Publishers, 1966), p. 175.

[18] *Ibid.*

[19] *Ibid.*, p. 176.

[20] *Ibid.*

[21] It is interesting to note, though, that in a book which proposes to deal with God in the context of Teilhard's evolutionary thought, the author shys away from tampering too much with God's "immutability." In *God Within Process* Eulalio Baltazar writes: "I am not ready to accept the view that God evolves because of my concern to safeguard what I believe is also quite biblical about God's eternity, namely, its immutability" (p. 114). In several other places it is clear that B. would not go as far as the process thinkers a la Whitehead: "Similarly, though God is the Fullness of Time, he does not grow or become" (p. 127).

The two images B. uses in several places to speak about God are a mother and the earth. He says: "Thus the mother does not grow or develop; the child does. Nor does the ground grow; the seed does (p. 127). Is it not obvious that in both instances there is real modification of both mother and ground, and that both are really changed somehow?

[22] Cf. Thomas Ommen, "The Hermeneutic of Dogma," *Theological Studies*, Vol. 36, No. 3 (June, 1975), p. 613.

[23] (New Haven, Conn.: Yale University Press, 1964), p. 41.

[24] *Ibid.*, p. 58.

[25] Burton Z. Cooper, *The Idea of God.* A Whiteheadian Critique of St. Thomas Aquinas' Concept of God. The Hague: Martinus Nijhoff, 1974), p. xiii. On this see also Leslie Dewart's *The Future of Belief*: "The hellenic cultural form of Christianity...has made it difficult for us to realize the difference between man's relations with the God of metaphysics and his relations with the God of the Christian religion" (p. 200).

26(Jena: Fromann, 1923), pp. 123-124.

27(London: Hodder and Stroughton, 1954), p. 3 ff.

28"Note Sur La Formule 'Ehyeh Aser Ehyeh,'" *Recherches de Science Religieuse*, 45, No. 1 (Jan-Mar., 1957), pp. 81, 86.

29*A Christian Theology of the Old Testament* (London: SCM Press Ltd., 1959), pp. 41-42.

30Ed. James Hastings (New York: Charles Scribner's Sons, 1906), Vol. II, p. 199.

Chapter 2

1Quoted by Charles Moore, "Professor Hocking and East-West Philosophy," *Philosophy, Religion, and the Coming World Civilization*, ed. Leroy S. Rouner (The Hague: Martinus Nijhoff, 1966), p. 351.

2Paul K. K. Tong, "A Study of Thematic Differences Between Eastern and Western Religious Thought," *Journal of Ecumenical Studies*, Vol. X (Spring, 1973), No. 2, p. 341.

3Thomas R. Blackburn, "Sensuous-Intellectual Complementarity in Science," in *The Nature of Human Consciousness*, ed. Robert E. Ornstein (San Francisco: W. H. Freeman Company, 1973), p. 29.

4Davidson, *op. cit.*, p. 199.

5Blackburn, *op. cit.*, p. 29.

6(London: SCM Press, Ltd., 1960), p. 208.

7Robert E. Ornstein, *The Psychology of Human Consciousness* (San Francisco: W. H. Freeman and Company, 1972), p. 12.

8Cf. Appendix A for further scientific information on the two hemispheres.

9Blackburn, *op. cit.*, p. 34.

[10] *Ibid.*, p. 35.

[11] *Ibid.*, p. 39.

Chapter 3

[1] Boman, *op. cit.*, p. 27.

[2] *Ibid.*, p. 31.

[3] *Ibid.*, p. 46.

[4] *Proceedings, op. cit.* pp. 139-140.

[5] *Ibid.*, pp. 48-49.

[6] *Ibid.*, p. 65.

[7] *Ibid.*, p. 67.

[8] *Ibid.*, p. 68.

[9] *Ibid.*, p. 106.

[10] *Ibid.*, p. 111.

[11] *Ibid.*, p. 112.

[12] (London: Collins, 1973), pp. 27, 37.

[13] Boman, *op. cit.*, p. 205.

[14] *Ibid.*, p. 121.

[15] Boman, *op. cit.*, p. 111.

[16] *Ibid.*, p. 121.

Chapter 4

[1] H. Wheeler Robinson, *Religious Ideas of the Old Testament*, p. 51, quoted by A.W. Argyle, *God in the New Testament* (London: Hodder and Stoughton, 1965), p. 14.

Footnotes

[2] *The Theology of the Old Testament*, trans. J. A. Baker (London: SCM Press Ltd., 1961), Vol. 1, p. 178.

[3] *Ibid.*, pp. 206-207.

[4] (London: Cambridge University Press, 1926), pp. 1, 3.

[5] Frank Michaeli, *Dieu A L'Image de L'Homme*. Etude de la notion anthropomorphique de Dieu dans l'Ancien Testament (Paris: Delachaux et Niestle, 1950), p. 152.

[6] Jurgen Moltmann, *The Crucified God* (London: SCM Press, Ltd., 1974), pp. 271-272.

[7] Hermann Schultz, *Old Testament Theology* (Edinburgh: T. & T. Clark, 1895), Vol. 1, p. 103.

[8] Eichrodt, *op. cit.*, pp. 211, 110.

[9] *Ibid.*, p. 213.

[10] *Ibid.*, p. 212.

[11] Eichrodt, *op. cit.*, p. 278.

[12] *Ibid.*

[13] *Ibid.*, p. 210.

[14] *Ibid.*

[15] *Ibid.*, p. 216.

[16] Argyle, *op. cit.*, p. 11.

[17] Gollwitzer, *op. cit.*, p. 155.

[18] Quoted by Vriezen, *op. cit.*, p. 173.

[19] Vriezen, *op. cit.*, p. 173.

[20] *Op. cit.*, p. 172.

[21] Argyle, *op. cit.*, pp. 14-15.

[22] Eichrodt, *op. cit.*, p. 206.

[23] *Ibid.*, p. 208.

[24] Gollwitzer, *op. cit.*, pp. 168-169.

[25] Davidson in *Dictionary, op. cit.*, p. 198.

[26] *Ibid.*

[27] Gollwitzer, *op. cit.*, p. 149.

[28] *Ibid.*, p. 169.

Chapter 5

[1] Eichrodt, *op. cit.*, pp. 219, 218.

[2] *Ibid.*, p. 218.

[3] *Prayer in the Apocrypha and Pseudoepigrapha*, A Study of the Jewish Concept of God (Philadelphia: Society of Biblical Literature and Exegesis, 1948).

[4] *Ibid.*, p. 71.

[5] *Ibid.*, p. 9.

[6] Quoted by Johnson, *op. cit.*, p. 72.

[7] *Ibid.*, p. 71.

[8] *Ibid.*, p. 72.

[9] *The Old Rabbinic Doctrine of God* (New York: KTAV Publishing House, Inc., 1968), p. 111.

[10] *Ibid.*, p. 56.

[11] Ethelbert Stauffer, "Theos," *Theological Dictionary of the New Testament*, eds. Gerhard Kittel and Gerhard Friedrich (Grand Rapids, Michigan: Wm. B. Eerdmans Publishing Co., 1968), p. 110.

[12] Marmorstein, *op. cit.*, p. 123.

[13] *Ibid.*, p. 70.

[14] *Ibid.*, p. 72.

[15] *Op. cit.*, p. 272.

[16] *Ibid.*, p. 273.

[17] Stauffer, *op. cit.*, p. 110.

[18] Grant, *op. cit.*, p. 3.

[19] Argyle, *op. cit.*, p. 9.

[20] *Ibid.*, p. 10.

[21] Arthur Cushman McGiffert, *The God of the Early Christians* (Edinburgh: T. & T. Clark, 1924), pp. 3-4.

[22] R. P. C. Hanson, *The Attractiveness of God*, Essays In Christian Doctrine (London: SPCK, 1973), p. 63.

[23] Robert Franks, "Passibility and Impassibility," *Encyclopedia of Religion and Ethics*, ed. James Hastings, Vol. IX, p. 658.

[24] *Op. cit.*, p. 16.

[25] Lukyn A. Williams, " 'My Father' in Jewish Thought of the First Century," *The Journal of Theological Studies* (Oct. 1929), XXXI, No. 121, p. 42.

[26] *Ibid.*, p. 43.

[27] *Ibid.*, p. 45.

[28] *Ibid.*, p. 47.

[29] *Ibid.*, p. 42.

[30] E. Mangenot, "Dieu (sa Nature D'Apres La Bible)," *Dictionnaire de Theologie Catholique*, IV, p. 1018.

[31] *Ibid.*, p. 1017.

[32] McGiffert, *op. cit.*, pp. 12-13. It is well to emphasize this aspect of Jesus' teaching about God since we tend so easily to get carried away by our sentimental notions of love. "In the Old Testament, as in the New, the Lord God, creator of heaven and earth, appears as a terrifying God—'it is a fearful thing to fall into the hands of the living God'—and also like a God who loves this creature man, whom He has made. His very essence was defined in the epistle of John: God is *agape*. But this *agape* is severe, because it is love, and love requires and demands justice. *Agape* is not complacency or weakness, nor is it willingness to allow man to degrade himself, but a stern demand, an infinite demand, for the sake of man, who is not called to become a pampered puppet, but rather a divine being, with God Himself." Cf. Tresmontant, *op. cit.*, p. 114.

[33] McGiffert, *op. cit.*, p. 19.

[34] *Ibid.*

[35] Grant, *op. cit.*, p. 3.

[36] Mangenot, *op. cit.*, p. 1023.

[37] *Op. cit.*, p. 5.

[38] Grant, *op. cit.*, p. 13.

[39] *Ibid.*, pp. 4-5.

[40] *Ibid.*

[41] *Ibid.*, p. 2.

[42] Hanson, *op. cit.*, p. 76.

[43] *Op. cit.*, p. 5.

[44] Hanson, *op. cit.*, p. 46.

[45] Grant, *op. cit.*, p. 110.

[46] *Ibid.*, p. 13.

Chapter 6

[1] *The Christian Platonists of Alexandria* (Oxford: The Clarendon Press, 1913), p. 25.

[2] *Gospel Message and Hellenistic Culture*, A History of Early Christian Doctrine Before the Council of Nicaea, Vol. Two, trans. John Austin Baker (Philadelphia: the Westminster Press, 1973), p. 326.

[3] Bigg, *op. cit.*, p. 31.

[4] Goodenough, *An Introduction To Philo Judaeus* (Oxford: Basil Blackwell, 1962), p. 12.

[5] *Philo*, Foundations of Religious Philosophy in Judaism, Christianity, and Islam, 4th ed. revised (Cambridge, Mass., Harvard University Press, 1968), Vol. 1, pp. 12-13. Also, for some excellent insights into Philo's bible cf. "La Bible de Philon: Les LXX," in Jean Danielou, *Philon D'Alexandrie* (Paris: Librairie Artheme Fayard), pp. 95-102.

[6] For these modifications of LXX cf. Danielou, *Philon, op. cit.*, pp. 97-102.

[7] *Gospel Message, Op. cit.*, p. 324.

[8] Gollwitzer, *op. cit.*, p. 154.

[9] Wolfson, *op. cit.*, p. 26. But Grant makes a very significant comment about Aristeas' method which shows us which way the wind was blowing: "Thus Aristeas insists on the inspiration of scripture in order to facilitate his adaptation of it to philosophy. *The ultimate ground of knowledge lies in philosophy, of which the Old Testament is a symbolical expression*" (emphasis added). Cf. *The Letter and the Spirit* (London: S.P.C.K., 1957), p. 32. The writings of Aristeas are dated about 100 B.C.

[10] Bigg, *op. cit.*, p. 35.

[11] Philo, *The Unchangeableness of God*, trans. F. H. Colson, Loeb Classical Library, Vol. III (Cambridge, Mass.: Harvard University Press, 1954). Following quotes from this work.

[12] Goodenough, *Introduction*, p. 97.

[13] Danielou, *Gospel Message*, p. 326.

[14] *Op. cit.*, p. 33.

[15] Wolfson, *op. cit.*, pp. 58-58.

[16] *Ibid.*, p. 60.

[17] Quoted by Goodenough, *Introduction*, p. 81.

[18] James Drummond, *Philo Judaeus*, the Jewish-Alexandrian Philosophy in its Development and Completion (London: Williams and Norgate, 1888), Vol. 1, p. 49.

[19] *Ibid.*, p. 51.
"One does not choose a 'Zeitgeist,' but the 'Zeitgeist' has us in its grip whether we like it or not. So it is, always has been, and always will be. The Fathers' insistence on God's unchangeability was caused by the philosophical 'Zeitgeist.' The 'Zeitgeist' made the Fathers read Platonic ontology into the Bible. Our own 'Zeitgeist' makes us ask for changeability, especially of the structures of society. Equally the 'Zeitgeist' makes us read this kind of changeability into the Bible. We need not be ashamed of this since we cannot help it. What we can do is make an effort to be critical not only of the Fathers and their 'Zeitgeist,' but also of ourselves and our 'Zeitgeist.'" Cf. E. P. Meijering, *God Being History*, Studies in Patristic Philosophy (Oxford: North-Holland Publishing Company, 1975), p. 150.

[20] *Introduction*, p. 87, 85.

[21] *Ibid.*, p. 87. Speaking of Philo's method, Grant also says, "God is immutable (Ex. 2:12); therefore passages ascribing passions to him must be allegorized. For though God is the creator he is not in any way anthropomorphic. Here Philo joins the philosophers." Cf. *Letter*, p. 34.

[22] Julius Guttman, *Philosophers of Judaism* (London: Routledge and Kegan Paul, 1964), p. 25.

[23] *Ibid.*, p. 28.

[24] Wolfson, *op. cit.*, p. 98.

[25] *Ibid.*, p. 111.

[26] *Ibid.*, p. 138.

[27] For the sake of comparison, read again the quote from Donceel, pp. 15-16.

[28] Wolfson, *op. cit.*, p. 138.

[29] Cf. Chapter 4, p. 68 ff. of present work.

Chapter 7

[1] Richard A. Norris. *God and World In Early Christian Theology*, A Study in Justin Martyr, Irenaeus, Tertullian and Origen (London: Adam and Charles Black, 1966), p. 6.

[2] *Ibid.*

[3] Cooper, *op. cit.*, p. 1.

[4] *Ibid.*

[5] *Ibid.*

[6] Norris, *op. cit.*, p. 31.

[7] *Ibid.*

[8] *Ibid.*

[9] *Ibid.*

[10] Moltmann, *op. cit.*, pp. 269-270.

[11] *Op. cit.*, p. 7.

[12] *A Handbook of Patrology*, trans. S. A. Raemers (London: 1947), p. 13.

[13] *Doctrine*, p. 13.

[14] Mozley, *op. cit.*, pp. 7-8.

[15] *Ibid.*

[16] Goodenough, *Justin Martyr*, pp. 123-124.

[17] Norris, *op. cit.*, p. 33.

[18] T. E. Pollard, "The Impassibility of God," *Scottish Journal of Theology*, VIII (1955), p. 357.

[19] Cooper, *op. cit.*, p. 2.

[20] Goodenough, *Justin Martyr*, p. 123.

[21] *Doctrine*, p. 33.

[22] Norris, *op. cit.*, p. 38.

[23] Mozley, *op. cit.*, p. 11.

[24] Norris, *op. cit.*, pp. 48-49.

[25] *Ibid.*

[26] *Ibid.*, p. 50.

[27] *Ibid.*, p. 53.

[28] *Ibid.*
Goodenough concludes his study of Justin's notion of God by saying that Justin only uses *apathes* of God in one passage (Apol. I, 25, 2), and that throughout this works "God is represented as stirred by emotions of many kinds." Justin reflects the uncritical attitudes of Hellenistic Judaism whose God was many-sided: "Like them Justin taught at one time that God was transcendent, unbegotten, impassive, perfect, self-contained, unmoved, unchanging, unnamed, the First Cause; at another time that He was the personal creator and sustainer of the universe; at another that He was the kind merciful Father who led errant individuals into faith

and saved them by His grace, or the dread God of righteousness whose final judgment awaited all men. Such a many-sided God was the God of the Wisdom Literature of the Hellenistic Jewish philosophers. . . ." Cf. *Justin Martyr*, p. 138.

[29] Mozley, *op. cit.*, p. 12.

[30] *Ibid.*, p. 14.

[31] The quotations from Athenagoras which follow are taken from Alexander Roberts and James Donaldson, editors, *The Ante-Nicene Fathers* (Grand Rapids, Mich.: Wm. B. Ferdmans Publishing Company, Reprinted, 1975), Vol. II. Quotes from Clement in Chapter 8 also from this volume.

[32] Quotations from Irenaeus also taken from above series, Vol. I.

[33] Mozley, *op. cit.*, p. 23.

[34] *Ibid.*, p. 23.

[35] *Ibid.*, p. 24.

Chapter 8

[1] Patrick J. Hamell, *Handbook of Patrology* (Staten Island, N.Y.: Alba House, 1966), p. 60.

[2] Danielou, *Gospel Message*, p. 308.

[3] Hans Von Campenhausen, *The Fathers of the Greek Church* (London: Adam and Charles Black, 1963), p. 30.

[4] Hamell, *op. cit.*, p. 63.

[5] *Clement of Alexandria*, A Study in Christian Platonism and Gnosticism (London: Oxford University Press, 1971), p. 232.

[6] Henry Chadwick, *Early Christian Thought and the Classical Tradition*, Studies in Justin, Clement, and Origen (London: Oxford University Press, 1966), p. 45.

[7] *Ibid.*, p. 40.

[8] *Ibid.*, p. 45.

[9] Lilla, *op. cit.*, p. 227.

[10] Mozley, *op. cit.*, p. 52.

[11] Lilla, *op. cit.*, p. 213.

[12] *Ibid.*

[13] *Ibid.*, p. 215.

[14] *Ibid.*, p. 199.

[15] Danielou, *Gospel Message*, pp. 326-327.

[16] E. F. Osborn, *The Philosophy of Clement of Alexandria* (London: Cambridge University Press, 1957), p. 27.

[17] Mozley, *op. cit.*, p. 55.

[18] Osborn, *op. cit.*, p. 28.

[19] *Ibid.*, p. 30.

[20] *Ibid.*

[21] Mozley, *op. cit.*, pp. 55-56.

[22] Lilla, *op. cit.*, p. 228.

[23] *Ibid.*, p. 217.

[24] Mozley, *op. cit.*, p. 57.

[25] *Gospel Message*, p. 343.

[26] *Op. cit.*, p. 31.

[27] *Gospel Message*, p. 342.

[28] *Op. cit.*, pp. 228-229.

[29] Mozley, *op. cit.*, p. 55.

[30] *Ibid.*

[31] Quoted by Mozley, p. 60.

[32] *Op. cit.*, p. 195.

[33] *Ibid.*, p. 196.

[34] Quoted by Mozley, p. 61.

[35] Quoted by Mozley, pp. 61-62.

[36] *Ibid.*

[37] *Ibid.*

Chapter 9

[1] Pollard, *op. cit.*, p. 354.

[2] Murray, *op. cit.*, pp. 51-52.

[3] (New York: Doubleday and Company, Inc., 1974), p. 16. Cf. also Jean Danielou *God and the Ways of Knowing* (New York: Meridian Books, 1957): "This mystery [of the Trinity] is the object of the theologian's attempt to arrive at definitions with the aid of analogies that are always inadequate, and yet not without some significance. These analogies may be of various kinds. For, if dogma is necessarily one, theologians may differ through the diversity of the conceptual instruments which they employ. The Church has always recognized this" (p. 210 ff.).

[4] Walter E. Stokes, S.J., "God For Today and Tomorrow," in Lewis S. Ford, ed., *Two Process Philosophers: Hartshorne's Encounter With Whitehead*, AAR Studies in Religion, No. 5.

[5] Dulles, *op. cit.*, p. 21.

[6] *Ibid.*, p. 24.

[7] *Ibid.*, p. 22.

[8] *Ibid.*, p. 23.

[9] *Ibid.*

[10] *Ibid.*, p. 27.

[11] *Ibid.*, p. 29.

[12] *Ibid.*

[13] Thomas S. Kuhn, quoted by Ornstein, *Psychology*, p. 3.

[14] One of the most influential of the process thinkers is John B. Cobb, Jr. His book include *A Christian Natural Theology, God and the World,* and *The Structure of Christian Existence.*

[15] "God's Reality: the Most Important Issue," *National Catholic Reporter*, June 23, 1972.

[16] Cobb, *Theology*, p. 144.

[17] *Process and Reality* (New York: Free Press, reprint, 1969), pp. 178-179.

[18] *Science In the Modern World* (New York: Free Press, reprint, 1967), p. 18.

[19] (Hartford, Conn.: Yale University Press, 1964), p. vii.

[20] A. Boyce Gibson, "The Two Strands in Natural Theology," *Process and Divinity*, ed. William L. Reese and Eugene Freeman (Lasalle: Open Court Publishing Co., 1964), p. 491.

[21] *Ibid.*

[22] Contents of this summary in Hartshorne, *op. cit.*, pp. 1-25, *passim.*

In a recent article which summarizes the dialogue between Tillich and process theologians, the author, Tyron Inbody, concludes: "The fundamental difference between Paul Tillich and the process theologians, then, is a religious one (p. 490). Tillich claims that authentic religious experience is an intuition of an unconditioned dimension in all being....For Hartshorne...the primary experience is the self as becoming in a world of becoming. There is no way to resolve this basically religious dispute...(p. 491)." Cf. "Tillich and Process Theology," *Theological Studies* (Sept. 1975), Vol. 36, No. 3, pp. 472-492. Are not these two views of reality simply the modern counterparts of the two basic views of reality we have been discussing in this book, Tillich's the Greek view and Hartshorne's the Hebrew? Would not the resolution to the problem be to hold them both in paradoxical tension, admitting the legitimacy of both?

[23] K. Kohler, *Jewish Theology* (New York: The Macmillan Co., 1923), p. 76.

[24] Heschel, *op. cit.*, pp. 3-11, *passim.*

[25] A Systematic Inquiry Into A Concept of Divine Passibility (The Hague: Martinus Nijhoff, 1974), p. 1. Leslie Dewart also gives voice to the neglect in this area of theology: "This book advances...the suggestion that the integration of Christian belief and contemporary experience must logically begin [with] the integration of the *concept of God* with contemporary experience. Surely if any part of the Christian faith must be in perfect harmony with everyday life it must be this. The direct treatment of the problem of everyday experience and the Christian belief *in God* has been relatively neglected...." Cf. *The Future of Belief* (New York: Herder and Herder, 1966), p. 37.

[26] Augustin Leonard, O.P., "Classical Philosophy and the Meaning of God," *Traces of God In a Secular Culture*, ed. George F. McLean, O.M.I. (Staten Island, N.Y.: Alba House, 1973), p. 250.

[27] Moltmann, *op. cit.*, p. 270.

[28] Vann, *op. cit.*, p. 59.

[29] *Op. cit.*, p. 79.

[30] Marmorstein, *op. cit.*, p. 155.

[31] *Ibid.*, p. 156.

[32] *Ibid.*

[33] *Ibid.*, pp. 73-74.

www.ingramcontent.com/pod-product-compliance
Lightning Source LLC
Chambersburg PA
CBHW051101160426
43193CB00010B/1271